EVANGELISM NOW

Ralph G. Turnbull, Editor

Baker Book House
Grand Rapids, Michigan

Copyright © 1972 by
Baker Book House Company

ISBN: 0-8010-8778-3
Library of Congress Card Catalog Number: 72-75551

Printed in the United States of America

Preface

In a book of this kind the editor and the publisher are indebted to the contributors for their willing service. When they were approached, each responded quickly and accepted the format to be followed. No restrictions were imposed upon the writers. Each was selected for his special gifts and qualifications. The aim has been to see the subject in the wide sweep of the need of our day. We cannot organize revival or renewal of the church by human methods devoid of divine inspiration and the work of the Holy Spirit. Thus the attempt has been made to have these brothers join together in a common bond of faith and conviction. They have expressed ideas and ideals, pointed out difficulties and dangers, and stressed the glory of the task as envisaged by each from his particular perspective on needs and opportunities. Thus there is unity in diversity; there is also encouragement for us all in the variety of methods of exposition. From the manifold ways and means of evangelism presented in this book, churches, laymen, and pastors may learn afresh something of the privilege and obligation of our God-given task—the evangelization of the world in our generation.

Contents

1. **What's the Big Idea?**
   A Theology of Evangelism
   Donald G. Miller 9

2. **Let's Keep Our Heads**
   Balance in Evangelism
   John Randolph Taylor 20

3. **What's It All About?**
   The Essence of Evangelism
   John W. Alexander 30

4. **Foundations Are Important**
   Biblical Foundations of Evangelism
   Samuel H. Moffett 38

5. **Preacher, Do Your Part**
   The Pastor-Preacher in Evangelism
   Harold J. Ockenga 48

6. **Let's March Abreast**
   The Congregation in Evangelism
   George E. Sweazey 58

7. **Let's Take to the Air**
   The Radio Opportunity in Evangelism
   Joel Nederhood 73

8. **Togetherness Has Advantages**
   The Evangelism of Mass Crusaders
   John Wesley White 81

9. **Let the Presses Roll**
   Evangelism Through Literature
   Sherwood E. Wirt 94

10. **Have You Caught the Spirit?**
    The Spirit of Evangelism
    Ralph G. Turnbull 103

    Bibliography 110

Contributors

Donald G. Miller Pastor, Laurinburg Presbyterian Church, Laurinburg, North Carolina, The Presbyterian Church in the US. Former President, Pittsburgh Theological Seminary, Pittsburgh, Pennsylvania, The United Presbyterian Church in the USA. Writings include *The Way to Biblical Preaching* and *Fire in Thy Mouth.*

John Randolph Taylor Pastor, Central Presbyterian Church, Atlanta, Georgia, The Presbyterian Church in the US. Writings include *God Loves Like That! The Theology of James Denney.*

John W. Alexander President, Inter-Varsity Christian Fellowship, Madison, Wisconsin. Leader of the Student Foreign Missions Fellowship, HIS Magazine, Nurses Christian Fellowship, Inter-Varsity Press and the 10,000 students annual convention, Urbana, Illinois.

Samuel H. Moffett Dean of the Graduate School and Professor of Historical Theology, The Presbyterian Seminary of the Presbyterian Church of Korea in Seoul. Missionary, Author. Writings include *Protestant Preaching in Lent.*

George E. Sweazey Professor of Homiletics, Princeton Theological Seminary, Princeton, New Jersey. Former Pastor, Webster Groves United Presbyterian Church, Webster Groves, Missouri. Director of Evangelism, The Presbyterian Church in the USA. Writings include *Effective Evangelism: The Greatest Work in the World.*

Joel Nederhood Preacher on "The Back to God Hour," national radio chain, The Christian Reformed Church, Grand Rapids, Michigan, successor to Peter Eldersveld, over three hundred radio stations and also TV. Writings include *The Church's Mission to the Educated American, God Is Too Much,* and *The Holy Triangle.*

John Wesley White Associate Evangelist to Billy Graham; Chancellor, Richmond College, Toronto, Canada. Writings include *Everywhere Preaching the Gospel.*

Sherwood E. Wirt Editor, *Decision* Magazine, worldwide circulation of four million, Minneapolis, Minnesota. Former President of the Evangelical Press Association. Writings include *The Social Conscience of the Evangelical* and *Love Song, A Fresh Translation of Augustine's Confessions.*

Ralph G. Turnbull Former Professor of Homiletics, Western Theological Seminary, Pittsburg, Pennsylvania, Pastor, First Presbyterian Church, Seattle, Washington. Writings include *A Minister's Obstacles; The Preacher's Heritage, Task and Resources;* and *Jonathan Edwards the Preacher.*

What's the Big Idea? 1

A THEOLOGY OF EVANGELISM

Donald G. Miller

One of the marks of the church in our time is a new awareness of the world. The church exists for the world, as a servant community living in the fellowship and by the power of a Servant Lord. The church has learned that the ministry of the church must be to the whole man in his total environment.

This awareness has had a strong effect on modern views of evangelism. The mission of the church is seen as being larger than that of helping individuals to go to heaven when they die. Rather, it is to smash all barriers that alienate men from one another, and to break all the shackles of this world that bind men's bodies and spirits, as well as to offer hope for the world to come. Evangelism, therefore, is seen in terms of two significant words, *reconciliation* and *freedom*. A genuine theology of evangelism is all-inclusive, dealing with the total human situation. It encompasses the whole range of man's reconciliation to God and to his fellowman, and thus concerns itself with the unshackling of men's bodies, minds, and spirits.

This has been said so often and so clearly by so many people that there seems to be quite general agreement on this point. But sweeping generalizations tend to become mere fads if they are not carefully examined. Therefore we must look deeper into the true meaning of the words *reconciliation* and *freedom*.

It is well to keep in mind that both of these words are frequently denuded of any distinctively Christian meaning. *Reconciliation* is often confined to the level of alienated human beings finally deciding to "get along" with each other. *Freedom,* too, is often secularized so that it refers solely to the realization of one's true humanity, to the right to participate in the decisions which affect one's own life, to man's ability to create his own future, or to the fullest realization of one's own potential.

Both *reconciliation* and *freedom*, then, are too often thought of merely in humanistic terms, in the jargon of sociology, economics, and politics. While we acknowledge that such usages are helpful to our understanding of their distinctively Christian meanings, we must not allow them to limit our perspective. The church has always out of necessity interacted with its environment. Although it is that community of faith which is called "out of the world" (John 17:6*), nevertheless it lives out its destiny "in the world" (17:11), and is sent "into the world" (17:18).

The words *reconcile* and *reconciliation* are not used frequently in the New Testament. The three Greek words so translated are used only thirteen times. The words themselves, therefore, are not decisive in helping us determine their meanings. Rather, the meanings must be found through the context of the passages in which they are used. In these passages, reconciliation is related to the following: Christ's act on "the cross" (Eph. 2:16); "the death of [God's] Son" (Rom. 5:10); God "no longer holding men's misdeeds against them" (II Cor. 5:19); and God making Christ "one with the sinfulness of men" (5:21). In the New Testament, reconciliation seems always to be closely related to atonement or redemption. The subjective interpersonal quality of the human experience of reconciliation, therefore, is mistakenly associated with the objective act of God in Christ; the reconciliation of sinful man with a holy God involves much more than may be seen in the reconciliation of estranged human beings to each other.

Furthermore, the passages in which the word *reconciliation* appears suggest that although it is ultimately a mutual thing, the mutuality is an outgrowth of an act of God that has no mutuality about it. Those who were "separate . . . strangers . . . without hope and without God . . . " (Eph. 2:12 ff.), "in his body of flesh and blood God has reconciled . . . to himself" (Col. 1:22). Man may receive the effects of this historic act, but he did not participate in it, nor did he contribute anything to it. "From first to last this has

*All references are to The New English Bible unless otherwise indicated.

been the work of God . . . [who] was in Christ reconciling the
world to himself . . . " (II Cor. 5:18, 19). "By his death we are
now put right with God" (Rom. 5:9a, TEV). Reconciliation is
even spoken of as that which we have "received" (Rom. 5:11,
TEV), which suggests it is the prior work of God on our behalf
that comes to us solely as a gift.

Very attractive and effective attempts have been made to negate
this. Some have argued that the word *reconciliation* should be
interpreted solely in terms of its "richly human core." But how
can we avoid facing the fact that the reconciliation of estranged
human beings, all of whom stand on the same level—sinners—is
something other than the reconciliation of sinful man with a holy
God? Paul hints at this when he says that there is no human
parallel by which to illustrate the love of God, because "God
shows his love for us in that while we were yet sinners Christ died
for us" (Rom. 5:8, RSV). This suggests that in dealing with the
New Testament view of reconciliation, we cannot really illustrate
it from human experience. Since the alienation of man from God
is "more bitter than anything that man can feel against man,"
because it involves such hate "as only holiness can produce," so
God's gift of reconciliation "is so great a miracle that it is strange,
remote, and alien to our natural ways of thinking and feeling"
(P. T. Forsyth, *The Work of Christ*, p. 28).

A doctor once said to me, "I work with sin every day, but I do
not have to *deal* with it." This, in my judgment, was a theologically sound distinction. God not only has to work with our sin; He
must *deal* with it before there can be any real reconciliation
between Him and us. And by the very nature of our sin, we cannot
assist Him in dealing with it. God must do this alone. James
Denney was not far from the mark when he wrote: "A finished
work of Christ and an objective atonement . . . are synonomous
terms. . . . Unless we can preach a finished work of Christ in
relation to sin, a . . . reconciliation or peace which has been
achieved independently of us . . . we have no real gospel for sinful
man at all" (*The Death of Christ*, p. 105).

God achieves reconciliation not as an arbitrator or an umpire in
disputes, nor as a diplomat or negotiator who seeks to bring an
agreement among competing interests. He is the reconciler solely
as redeemer through His Son. The distinctive role of the church in
being a reconciling community, then, is to confront men with the
good news that God has already "broken down the enmity which

stood like a dividing wall" between men, bringing their mutual
hostility to an end "through the cross" (Eph. 2:14-16). It is to
remind men that they may be truly reconciled to each other *only*
as they are first reconciled "to God" (v. 16). It is to invite men
to respond in faith to the fact that "*he* is himself our peace,"
because "through *him* we both alike have access to the Father in
the one Spirit," so that we may become "fellow citizens with
God's people, members of God's household" (2:14-20). The role
of the church is not merely to try to reconcile men for citizenship
in this world, but to summon them into God's new order created
in Christ, whereby they may be "rescued . . . from the power of
darkness and brought . . . safe into the kingdom of his dear Son,
by whom we are set free and our sins are forgiven" (Col. 1:13, 14,
TEV).

This last passage, with its reference to freedom, leads quite
naturally into a look at the New Testament view of freedom, for
here freedom is set in the framework of God's redemptive work
through Christ for the forgiveness of sins; indeed, freedom is here
synonomous with *the forgiveness of sins.* As we shall later see in
more detail, however much the New Testament doctrine of freedom may have implications for man's social, economic, and political existence, these implications must be worked out by Christian
ethicists against the background of the deeper theological dimension—man's true predicament, which robs him of his freedom, and
God's act in Christ, which restores to man his true humanity. It is
necessary to stress this at present, inasmuch as the church seems to
be in danger here, as elsewhere, of losing its distinctive role in
society and becoming just another agency for human betterment.
There is, of course, nothing wrong with being an agency for
human betterment and the church is incomplete when it is not
that. But it is much more incomplete if it becomes only that! For
then it is joining in an exercise in futility: in poulticing the surface
manifestations of a deep infection rather than dealing radically
with man's real need.

If the church is to remain God's kingdom on earth, and in a
genuine sense be "for the world," it may have to do so by quite
consciously resisting the world at this point. The world's call to
the church to join in its emancipation may be the call Jesus
refused in His temptation; it may be the call of the thief on the
cross whose demand that Jesus solve his problem at the superficial
level of political release was answered with silence. The church

may also have to resist those within its own fellowship who seem to deal with the problem of freedom in terms that do not plumb the depths of the New Testament faith.

An example of the challenge from within the church to divert it from its true task is an article in which a churchman suggests that it will not be long before theological seminary training will be shortened to about an eighteen-month grooming of a sort of sociological task force. He also suggests that knowledge and awareness of God's presence will be a thing of the past; that there will be little, if any, stress on belief in Jesus as divine Lord and Saviour; that sermons will make little mention of God, Jesus Christ, the Bible, the Holy Spirit, or the church; and that belief in prayer, the Scriptures, and the preaching of the Word will be all but extinct ("Pinpointing the Issue—The Ministry for the '70's," *Trends,* September, 1968). If this happens, the church will be powerless to give men true freedom.

Such views do not reckon with the deep sickness of human nature; they do not realistically assess the true human predicament. We should have no quarrel, of course, with a Christian "humanism" that places the Christian on the side of true human values. Nor, for that matter, should we quarrel with a non-Christian humanism in so far as its aims are concerned. But we cannot and may not accept the theory that humanistic goals may be ultimately achieved by forces generated purely within man. Such a humanism is man's rebellion against and alienation from God. This is man's slavery! How can that which produced man's slavery set him free from it?

In the first chapter of Romans, Paul analyzes the human predicament and finds that it arises because of man's refusal to acknowledge God as God; this leads to failure in rendering Him gratitude and encourages man to trust in his own wisdom. Paul sees this as the negation of man's humanity. All efforts to possess a self-contained freedom, to find the meaning of life through his own wisdom, and to build a worthy human society without God are self-defeating, for they are a denial of man's essential nature.

Much modern theology seems to define freedom as man's true humanity in political, sociological, or economic terms. But according to the New Testament, man's true humanity is to know himself a child of God.

For the Christian to deal with freedom apart from God's redemptive work in Jesus Christ, or to hope that he can minister to

man's real needs by efforts at social betterment alone, without the
preaching of the gospel, is not only theologically questionable but,
in the end, self-defeating. There are men who have all their civil
rights, who know no restrictions on their freedom from political,
economic, or social pressures, yet who do not know what freedom
in the New Testament sense is—freedom from themselves as
prisoners of sin and death! Merely enlarging this group through
social or political means does not fulfill the "ministry of reconciliation." The source of our bondage is the self-centeredness of our
existence instead of obedient acknowledgment of God and His will
for us. Freedom can be ours only when we have dealt with the
source of our slavery.

A survey of the use of the words for "freedom" in the New
Testament would seem to bear this out. The writers seldom meant
political liberty, except to suggest that it is not what is meant by
Christian freedom. At the time of Jesus' birth, the righteous
remnant were "looking for the liberation of Jerusalem" (Luke
2:38). At the time of His death, His disciples "had been hoping
that he was the man to liberate Israel" (Luke 24:21). But neither
Jerusalem nor Israel were liberated from Rome; they were de-
stroyed by her. The bondage from which Israel was to be released
is variously referred to as: "the commands of sin" (Rom. 6:22);
"the law of sin and death" (8:2); "wickedness" (Titus 2:14); "the
empty folly of your traditional ways" (I Peter 1:18); "the domain
of darkness" (Col. 1:13); "sin" (John 8:34; Rom. 6:17, 20 f.;
Heb. 9:15). Prideful human will at the center of reality, is sin. It is
this *from* which men must be delivered.

And *to* what are men set free? Certainly not to do as they
please. They are now "bound to the service of God" (Rom. 6:22);
they are "slaves of Christ," whose joy it is to "serve the Lord"
(Eph. 6:6, 7); they are "slaves in God's service" (I Peter 2:16);
they are "slaves . . . to the service of righteousness" (Rom. 6:17,
18); they are "servants to one another in love" (Gal. 5:13); they
are set free to become members of "one body . . . in the one
Spirit" (I Cor. 12:13); they are free to become "one person in
Christ Jesus" (Gal. 3:28), those among whom "Christ is all, and is
in all" (Col. 3:11).

And *how* are they set free? They are set free by "the Son"
(John 8:36); by "Christ" (Gal. 5:1); by "the Spirit of the Lord"
(II Cor. 3:17); by "the life-giving law of the Spirit" (Rom. 8:2);
by Christ "who sacrificed himself for us" (Titus 2:14); by the

"precious blood . . . the blood of Christ" (I Peter 1:19); by "God's free grace alone, through his act of liberation in the person of Christ Jesus" (Rom. 3:23, 24); by "God's act" in "Christ Jesus . . . in [whom] we are . . . set free" (I Cor. 1:30); by "the shedding of his blood" (Eph. 1:7); by being "rescued . . . from the domain of darkness" by God's Son, "in whom our release is secured and our sins forgiven" (Col. 1:13, 14); by Jesus' "death" (Heb. 9:15).

Does not all this suggest that where the church speaks of freedom it is called to herald the truth that men are bound by an enslavement they can never conquer; that however desirable freedom from the oppression of external circumstances is, such freedom can never take the place of that freedom from sin? If our wrestling were merely against "flesh and blood" or if Christ's kingdom were merely of "this world" we might then take the sword, or, conversely, use the powers of passive resistance to break the shackles that bind men. But our task moves in a much deeper dimension. As Paul Minear wrote, one of the tasks of the church is "to announce the opportunity of freedom to men who were still in bondage. But underneath this task [lies] a more far-reaching one—that of serving as Christ's agents in bringing into subjection the principalities which keep men in bondage" (*The Kingdom and the Power,* p. 190).

The unique task of the church is to help men become free from the "principalities and powers" that utilize human history for their destructive ends. And no easy view of freedom will do. We shall have to do more profound thinking to discover the "relevance" of the church in this time of world history lest we abandon our unique task in disillusionment and self-defeat.

There are at least three points related to this discussion about which the church ought to be cautious. The first concerns the struggle for freedom in the social order. It hardly needs documenting that many of the church's own adherents are defining *relevance* in the church only in terms of becoming an instrument in the solution of the problems of poverty, race, war, ignorance, and prejudice. Few of us wish to argue that the church should be aloof from, or unconcerned about, these problems. But should the church's concern with these issues be of no deeper quality than that of other "action" groups? And if these problems fail to be resolved, does the church have no word of hope to direct to that failure? On the other hand, if the hopes for human justice were wholly fulfilled, would the work of the church then be done? Suppose poverty, racism, war, ignorance, and prejudice were no more; would the word of the gospel no longer be needed? There are depths in human nature to which the gospel speaks that are unrepresented by the revolutionary social, political, and economic movements of our day.

And while advocates of a theology of relevance battle with the evil entrenched in the social order, can the church abdicate its function of reminding them that all power tends toward corruption, and that we must offer men inner freedom from the powers of darkness through the liberating work of Jesus Christ? Without this freedom, the exorcising of the demons they seek to cast out could open the way for more demons to enter, leaving the last state worse than the first. To take power from some so that others may have it, but to leave all outside the sphere of Christ's mastery of that which is demonic in all power, is a reshuffling of personnel that will only perpetuate a corrupt situation. The issue is not who is to rule and who is to be ruled, but whether the rulers and the ruled exercise their functions responsibly. If the advocates of relevance in the church preach Christ's freedom to the needy, they will be doing much to solve the problems of society. Then they can more successfully resolve political, social, and economic problems.

A second issue the church should be concerned with is the current struggle for freedom in personal living represented in the so-called new morality and situation ethics. We must undertake a more thorough analysis of this topic. For example, can we be so sure that our efforts to avoid "legalism" may not result in a new bondage to other forms of the demonic where Christ's Lordship is unacknowledged, rather than in genuine Christian freedom? We must be aware of the realm of the demonic where God is no longer acknowledged as God, nor praised, and where man's own wisdom is put in place of God's will for man. Some of the extreme illustrations of the validity of the "new morality" are suspect in that they seem to adopt "self-understanding" or "self-realization" as the measure of the good. How this is to be equated with the Biblical measure—the glory of God—is not clear. Furthermore, when one helps another to an alleged "self-realization" by a process that is self-gratifying, such as offering sexual intercourse as a "meaningful" experience, one wonders whether such acts are those of men free to acknowledge God as God, or whether they are mere manifestations of slavery to the "flesh."

The only true path to personal freedom is through slavery to Jesus Christ. Regarding personal ethics, the truth is that both we and the situations we face are subject to the temptations of the demonic. We can be liberated only by Him who has conquered the demonic and is now Lord. He is the touchstone of ethical decisions. As Dietrich Ritschl has written, " . . . while contextual ethics seeks the criterion for ethics in the situations . . . ," the better approach is to seek " . . . the criterion in Him. *He* opens the eyes of those who seek and the ears of those who listen to the understanding of the situation" (*Memory and Hope,* p. 200).

The third issue deals with the struggle for freedom in the institutional church, or, as sometimes is the case, *from* the institutional church. We need to distinguish between the freedom with which Christ sets us free, and the freedom which is often merely a form of self-assertion. Here again it would seem to be an oversimplification to identify the demonic with institutions *per se,* or to define freedom as emancipation from institutional involvement. Secular freedom is often defined as having autonomous authority over one's own actions; however, institutions do have a valid function. History indicates that institutions help to maintain an orderly continuity with the past. History also demonstrates that valuable though justice is (and how could there be any justice without institutions?), men can live without justice, but they cannot live without order.

Similarly, there are those whose conception of freedom in the church is escape from all forms of institutional life. But the New Testament does not support this standpoint. It does not support the idea that demonic powers exist only in the "establishment" and that enlightened and dedicated individuals who dream of eliminating the effects of sin are "free" because they have broken with the establishment. The churches at Rome and at Corinth both had institutional defects, and both had members who sought to bend the institution to their own view of things, thinking that freedom lay in changing the church, or otherwise in abandoning it. Paul saw clearly that their protest could be as demonic as the things they were protesting.

The question of the value of institutions and protests against them must be solved at the point where Christ sets men free. The question He helps us phrase is: Does the functioning of the institution represent corporate acknowledgment of God and His praise and His wisdom, or corporate human glorification, pride, and self-deceit? This same question must be raised in regard to protesters against the institution. Paul's word to both was: "We ... ought ... not to please ourselves" (Rom. 15:2, RSV). This means that we do "no more pass judgment on one another, but rather decide never to put a stumbling-block or hindrance in the way of a brother" (Rom. 14:13, RSV), and that we "pursue what makes for peace and for mutual upbuilding" (Rom. 14:19, RSV). True freedom from the demonic in the institutional life of the church is to be found, not in exchanging epithets with each other or in passing judgment on our brothers (practices which are far too common in church assemblies and publications today), but in mutual acknowledgment that "each of us shall give account of himself to God" (Rom. 14:12, RSV).

Nor does freedom lie in abandoning the institution with an air of superiority and condescension, rejoicing at the privilege of weakening it more; rather, freedom is found in seeing to it that in our corporate struggle to find the will of Christ, we "give no opportunity to the devil" (Eph. 4:27, RSV). If "Christ loved the church and gave himself for her" (5:25), we shall not go far wrong in loving her ourselves. Even if the institutional church should go down, we would do well, as did Jeremiah, to invest in her future. Paul insisted that it was "through the church" that "the manifold wisdom of God" was to "be made known to the principalities and powers in the heavenly places" (Eph. 3:10, RSV). And this church was no ideal or authentic church imagined by someone dissatisfied with the church as it was. It was the concrete, historical reality seen in the poor, struggling, quarreling, sinning churches of Rome, Corinth, Colossae, Laodicea, Thessalonica, and so on. It is through the fellowship of the saints that we discover, in forgiveness and hope, who we are, what our past is, what our present task is, and what our future is.

I conclude with some words of a letter from Professor Roland M. Frye of the University of Pennsylvania:

> I am ... much concerned about the present state of the church, which seems so often to be unable to speak the authentic and classical doctrines with force and conviction. There are many reasons to feel that the present temper of the world is quite open to the ancient Christian beliefs, and yet, so few theologians are able or

willing to present these. The prophetic and social ministry are terribly important, and I am sure that you are aware of my convictions of that importance, yet I often fear that prophetic and social comments are about all that the present generation of theologians and clergymen seem able to deliver. It is important, but it is not enough. The sociologists can do as much.

In our search for a theology of evangelism, let us continue to join forces with those who oppose injustice and racism and who seek to improve the lot of man on earth. But let us at the same time continue "to speak the authentic and classical doctrines with force and conviction." Only thus may we be genuinely and abidingly relevant.

Let's Keep Our Heads 2

BALANCE IN EVANGELISM

John Randolph Taylor

"And [has] bestowed on him the name which is above every name, that at the name of Jesus every knee should bow, in heaven and on earth and under the earth, and every tongue confess that Jesus Christ is Lord, to the glory of God the Father" (Phil. 2:9-11*).

The New Testament dares to say that Jesus Christ is the central figure in history. Paul declared that "I decided to know nothing among you except Jesus Christ" (I Cor. 2:2); and in this preoccupation with one figure Paul is not alone, for the whole of the New Testament supports him in this. Since the New Testament was written, the church has concentrated on this single person. In Him God is declared; in Him humanity is known; in Him our responsibility is seen; in Him our redemption has drawn near; in Him purpose and meaning have been given to life. There is need, therefore, for every person, particularly those who are called by the name Christian, to have a conscious Christology, a conscious awareness of who this Christ is.

The writers of the New Testament had a variety of ways of speaking about Jesus Christ. They called Him Messiah, they called Him Master, they called Him Healer, Teacher, Friend, Savior, Leader, Example, Rabbi, Lord, Priest, Prophet, King, Shepherd, Door, Bread, Fountain, Light, Way, Truth, Life, Head, Pioneer,

*References are to the Revised Standard Version.

20

Perfecter, Alpha, and Omega. These are all images which are used by the New Testament, and all of them refer to the single, central figure of the Christ.

The church has taken two of these titles and considers them to be holding the primary truths about the Christ. These words are *Lord* and *Savior*. When a person joins the church, he declares that Jesus Christ is his Savior and his Lord. The terms *Lord* and *Savior*, throughout the history of the church, have been the twin pillars of our Christology.

The fact is, however, that for many centuries and certainly in our own, we have centered our attention upon one of them to the exclusion of the other. The concept upon which our Christology has concentrated is the concept of Jesus as our Savior. This is the way we think of Him, talk of Him, and present Him to the world. This is because we have inherited our framework for under-standing who He is; sometimes, through concentration upon this framework, we have not realized the nature of our inheritance, and therefore not looked at it honestly to consider where it has taken us.

We are sons and daughters of the Protestant Reformation, and in the Reformation, Luther was still asking the basicly medieval, Romanist question, "How can I propitiate an angry God?" The presupposition was that God was angry and that man could be made aware of His anger. Salvation was based on the concept that man must make propitiation. Calvin organized this into an orderly process in his *Institutes*, centering upon salvation in Christ. Later, Wesley emphasized its subjective quality in terms of feeling the experience of salvation. The Christ of Protestantism, however, has always remained the same medieval Christ with which Luther himself was grappling in the Reformation. Luther came to the discovery that indulgences do not make propitiation real for man, but that the experience of forgiveness through faith itself does. But the question basically was the question of propitiation. This is still so today, so that our Christ is still the suffering Christ, now alive and let loose in the world!

As a minister of the gospel, I preach occasionally on such a text as "By grace you have been saved through faith; and this is not of your own doing, it is the gift of God." This I must and will preach, for this is a part of the truth expressed in the song, "Rock of Ages": "Nothing in my hands I bring, Simply to Thy cross I cling." But this is only part of the truth, and the result from such a sermon is inevitably that those who sit in the pews will leave the sanctuary feeling fairly useless. In the week before them they have decisions to make, neighbors to argue with or befriend, children to discipline and to love, office workers to associate with, frustrations and tempers to put down; but somehow salvation seems to have nothing really to do with any of these things. Cities go up in flames, labor and management quarrel, the cold war continues, injustice, war, and pollution persist, and to many Christians salvation seems unrelated. It seems to be a spiritual transaction in which everything is done for him. The result has been described by Pierre Burton, a Canadian journalist who has written an uncomfortable book entitled *The Comfortable Pew,* in which he indicates that the church has caught a contagious disease. He says, "The virus that has weakened the church is apathy." Too many persons have the feeling that since there is nothing they can do, they will simply do nothing about what is taking place in their own lives and in the world. If, after all, everything has been done for me, then I have no responsibility beyond the acceptance of that which has been done.

This emphasis on the grace of God would seem, furthermore, to be the strategy by which we seek to bring God's Word to the world. In view of this, we must ask whether since medieval times this actually has been an effective way of communicating the variety and diversity of the truth and centrality of Christ. And further, beyond the pragmatic question regarding the effectiveness of this method, there is a deeper question: is it in fact true to the full-orbed revelation of God in Jesus Christ which we find in the New Testament?

Our single-minded concentration upon the concept of Jesus as our Savior has put us out of balance. In the first place, it centers upon *sin.* We begin with sin, because—after all—if we are to come in at the door of our Savior, then we will have to feel a need for a Savior. Inevitably, we begin to talk about sin. Luther taught that Christ's redemption was an attack upon four basic realities and, therefore, preaching the gospel begins with one of these realities: hell, the law, the devil, or the experience of sin. The fact is that this is still where we begin as we try to lead people to an understanding of what it means to accept Jesus as our Savior.

Listen to Billy Graham sometime and discover with which of the four he begins: hell, the law, the devil, or the experience of sin—he always starts with one. Our most popular evangelist and he is caught in a logical box!

This means that the minister or the evangelist who seeks to preach the good news must, by the very nature of his theology and of our expectations, first of all preach the bad news. He must tell us, in effect, that the world is going to hell. He must tell us that we ourselves are part of the world that is going to hell. He must make the choice we have unmistakably clear: either we will lay hands of faith on Jesus Christ and His promises, or we will surely be consumed in one way or another by the forces of evil. This means that the evangelist has the peculiar position of, first of all, not being an evangelist at all, for an evangelist declares the good news. He really has to start out as a "malangelist," declaring the bad news; then people will be ready to understand the good news.

This oftentimes leads to a kind of induced sense of sin that can be artificial. A man may recognize that he gets relief from his own guilt complexes by hearing how bad he is and how bad the world is. The ground is then prepared in his own psychological makeup and he is ready to believe and want some good news. After all, if the situation really is this bad, then he must hold to something that is ultimate; thus the gospel comes like an ark on the tossing waves into which he is sinking.

A young teen-ager, faced with the perplexities of life, sex, relationships to the family, his vocation, study, and all the rest, feels this insecurity in a very intense way. The result is that many of us have come out of the traumas of our own puberty into an understanding of Jesus as Savior. This fact raises the question for us whether there are adequate standards for the mature faith needed once we have developed beyond our teens. For some Christians, returning continually to that early experience of trauma and relief and telling others of their experiences seem to satisfy a psychological need. They have had a traumatic shift in emotions whereby they understood both their sin and Jesus as Savior. At the same time there are many others who have been made to feel guilty because somehow they have not gone through that trauma, and they are left to rake over the coals of their lives, wondering if there is not something essential which they have missed, hoping that somehow there is some little place within the life of the church where they can serve, even though they do not really feel fit.

In addition, we have to recognize that not only does our

traditional approach to theology force us to concentrate first on sin, thus inducing a feeling of guilt and embarrassment, but we have also brought with it the tremendous indifference of a large proportion of the world today. After all, today's man does not start with the recognition of his sin. He may come to that place, but he does not start there. A hymn written in 1862 has a verse which reads, "Art thou weary, art thou languid, art thou sore distressed?" Modern man's answer to the questions in that archaic phrasing is No. He feels that technology has given him power, and he is not "languid"; he may feel frustrated, he may feel insecure, but these antiquated phrases do not describe the nature nor the depth of his predicament. Such concepts as original sin and the fires of hell simply leave many modern minds cold. Confronted with such indifference, the church can do two things. It can say, "Their indifference is their own judgment upon them," or it can say, "There is something wrong with what we are saying." The church could recognize that somehow by focusing on one particular doorway into the truth of the gospel, we have not been fair to the full-orbed nature of that gospel.

In fact, I wonder if, in this regard, we have been truthful about our own experiences. Is it not true that for many of us the experience of repentance came out of and after the experience of faith; that confessions of sin and of need and the acceptance of Jesus as our Savior really came long after we tried hopefully, faithfully, to commit ourselves to Him as our Lord? By preaching only Jesus as Savior and diminishing the great New Testament truth of the Lordship of Christ, we have failed to recognize that most of us actually seek to follow in faith, seek to obey, seek to be His disciples and fail utterly. Then, in the process of failing, in the process of coming up against the demands of Jesus Christ we begin to sense our own need. Modern man likes to think of himself as being pretty well off, and he continues to think this of himself until finally he runs into Someone who is so true and so right, so honest, good, strong, meek, mighty, and wise. Then he sees himself for who he really is. In our work we have urged people not even to draw near to Jesus until they had come through the doors of consciousness of sin, repentance, confession, and then salvation; then we have expected the remainder of their lives to be a pure pathway in which they obeyed the Lordship of Christ. Yet the experience of any of us has not very likely been thus. And it does not appear to have been so in the experiences of the writers of the New Testament. Their great cry was that Jesus is Lord.

In the second place, to look upon Jesus as only our Savior causes us to *center upon self.* It makes Him *our* possession and we become the central factor. All of God's revelation, from Abraham down to Jesus and Paul and John, was directed toward "little ole me." It makes *me* the focus of attention and not Christ as Lord. In the process, Jesus is not our Lord; we become the lords of Jesus. This is the ultimate seduction. We do not put ourselves at His use; we begin to use Him for ourselves. Instead of His being our Advocate, we become His advocates, trying to convince others of what He has done for us. Instead of His interceding for us, we seek to intercede for Him. Instead of His grasping us, we grasp Him for ourselves, losing the balance which the New Testament always had, that Jesus is not only our Savior but also our Lord.

Thus you find a man who says quite piously that as he drives to town he prays to Jesus for a parking place and when he gets to his destination, sure enough, Jesus has provided one. Or another who says that since he has "given his life to Jesus" his sales contracts have spiraled upward. Do you see what that is saying? Jesus is our servant—busy finding us parking places or clients. By concentrating sole attention upon the Saviorhood of Christ, we are in danger of making ourselves the lords of Jesus.

Of course, in the process of concentrating exclusively upon His Saviorhood, we think of ourselves as being tremendously advantaged, and the rest of the world simply not as fortunate as we are. This satisfies a great human need to be "in," and fosters an indifference toward the problems of others. With the support of this emphasis upon Saviorhood the pain, hunger, injustice, and loneliness which others feel can be ignored. Concern is expressed that the church not meddle in matters of slums, etc., but rather simply preach salvation. Christ then becomes a kind of external bonus to those who are prosperous enough to have had time to listen to what we have preached. This Christ seems far removed from the Christ of the New Testament. Jesus and His cross and resurrection are made to appear as an escape hatch into eternity for ourselves.

This self-centeredness has seeped into our songs and into our bones. At youth conferences we used to love to sing "In the Garden." Listen to what it taught us: "And He walks with *me* and

He talks with *me,* and He tells *me I* am His own. And the joy we share, as we tarry there, *none other* has ever known." Now we did not consciously concentrate on ourselves, but those are the words we sang and their message to our psychological needs is perfectly clear. The danger inherent here is that this kind of reference to self is half-true. His saving grace is experienced by us as individuals, but our problem comes in realizing that He is not just *our* Savior. If we leave it at that we make the whole experience of faith and repentance center ultimately upon ourselves.

In the third place, this approach to faith *centers upon weakness.* It raises the unavoidable question whether in the process of speaking exclusively of the Saviorhood of Christ, we have not appealed to man's weakness instead of to his strength. What is needed today is something which speaks to man in his strength. Bonhoeffer speaks of man "come of age," or of man "in his maturity," or man "with strength in his hands," and he saw that strength exploited by a man like Hitler. When we think in terms of the force and power and strength and capacity for influence that is alive today, we need to recognize that the Saviorhood of Christ is pointed directly toward man's weakness. Our presentation of the gospel is aimed at certain characteristics of the personality—the receptive, the reflective, the passive. But there is an entirely different set of human attitudes that is a part of every person. These are the other tendencies—the aggressive, the assertive, the positive. But how does one speak to man in strength? Well, speak in the terms of the New Testament: Jesus is Lord. Man will come to service and to witness, not by a single concentration upon Saviorhood but by a balanced understanding of the revelation of God in Jesus Christ.

We must not substitute justification by feeling for justification by faith. We must not forget that faith has to do with obedience, and that obedience has to do with deeds. Faith is the practical commitment of the self to Christ in concrete and real deeds. It is the willingness to act and to be, and not just to need or to say. Unfortunately, we have restricted our freedom in the process of our limited focus. We need desperately to recapture in our age the New Testament cry that Jesus is Lord, for by our continued concentration on just His Saviorhood, we inevitably develop a kind of "in-group" of those who have had the experience, and an "out-group," those who hang along, who will not take major responsibility because they feel that they have nothing that qualifies them. The third group is the great mass of humanity who are forgotten, those outside the church.

A look at the New Testament should tell us that this is not the pattern of the early Christian Church. A further look will give us some interesting information. The word *Lord,* referring to Jesus, is used in the New Testament 634 times. The word *Savior,* referring to Jesus, is used 24 times. If we are going to take the Bible seriously, it would seem appropriate to reappraise our emphases.

We must, therefore, reconsider whether our preoccupation with the Saviorhood of Christ has not been counter-productive, both in our practice and in our proclamation. Furthermore, on a deeper level, we must face the genuine possibility that one of the reasons our gospel is not heeded may be the fact that it is simply not the full gospel.

We need to insist in all that we do and say that Christ is not only Savior, but He is also Lord. He is God's radical demand upon us and not just God's open gift to us. *Kurios Jesu!*—that is the New Testament cry.

It is the earliest Christian creed:

> No one can say "Jesus is Lord," except by the Holy Spirit.—I Cor. 12:3

> Every knee should bow . . . and every tongue confess that Jesus Christ is Lord.—Phil. 2:10, 11

> Confess with your lips that Jesus is Lord and believe in your heart that God raised him from the dead.—Rom. 10:9

> God has made him both Lord and Christ, this Jesus whom you crucified.—Acts 2:36

> What we preach is not ourselves, but Jesus Christ as Lord, with ourselves as your servants for Jesus' sake.—II Cor. 4:5

When the New Testament uses the word *Lord* it has a depth and a breadth of meaning inherited from both Greek and Jewish thought. The Greeks thought of its meaning in connection with ownership, and it referred to legal power, responsibility, or possession. It had been used in Greek mythology in reference to deity, in the role of commander or ruler. It was regarded as the absolute opposite of slave. In Roman times it came to be used in reference to Caesar. It was the symbol of a supreme power, to whom was due supreme loyalty.

In Jewish thought it had come to take the place in the transla-
tions of YHWH, the untranslatable tetragrammaton, the unspeak-
able name of God Himself. Says Kittel's *Theological Word Book of
the New Testament:*

> The God to whom the Canon bears witness is called "Lord" because
> He is there shown to be the exclusive holder of power over the
> cosmos and all men, the Creator of the world and the Master of life
> and death. The term "Lord" is thus a summation of the beliefs of
> the Old Testament. It is the wholly successful attempt to state what
> God is, what the Holy One means in practice for men, namely, the
> intervention of a personal will, with approximately the pregnancy
> and binding force which constitute the distinctive mark of the name
> YHWH.

Both the Greek and the Jewish thought forms are combined in
the affirmation of the New Testament that Jesus, the incarnate
Christ, with the power of His death upon Him, and in the glory of
His resurrection victory, is Lord.

Over what is Jesus the Lord? He is Lord in one's own life. In
your life and in mine, He is Lord of all. Lord of time, wants,
leisure, needs, home, love, work, play, politics, investments, relationships, patriotism, instincts, attitudes, and actions.

> Who answers Christ's insistent call
> Must give himself, his life, his all.
> Christ claims him wholly for His own;
> He must be Christ's and Christ's alone.

When a man commits his whole personality, his style of life and
his system of values to the Lordship of Christ, then he begins the
exciting discipline of being a disciple. Stumbling and falling in the
process of his developing commitment, he becomes conscious of
his own incapacity, and genuine repentance begins. One comes to
sense the Saviorhood of Christ in the light of His Lordship as He
calls us to the daily renewal of faith and repentance, to the daily
task of obedience to Him, and to the daily following of Him into
the unknown and the unknowable, apart from Him. His Lordship
and His Saviorhood become living realities as we grow in our
understanding that our Lord is mighty to save.

Jesus is Lord in the church. In the light of His Lordship, the
church can never be that upon which we scribble our own preju-
dices. We are not central to its life—He is. It is His body, His bride,
His household of faith, His family, His people. We talk about the
church of our choice, but the New Testament talks about the

church of His choice. We need this correct emphasis in the church today.

Robb McNeill in his book, *God Wills Us Free,* tells of the ruling elder who spoke in the heat of an emotional debate about the church's responsibility for the life of a city in Alabama. Someone had proposed that perhaps the gospel demanded a certain action by the session, to which the ruling elder replied, "To hell with the gospel, we have got to save this church!" That blunt statement is more typical of our attitude toward the church than we like to admit, for somehow we have become convinced that the church is ours to save. We are guilty of ecclesiolatry, worshiping the church and viewing it as big business without regard to the fact that it is His and not ours. Ruling elders, deacons, Sunday school teachers, advisors, planners, community strategists, ministers and parishioners in the church's public life and private service all need to be reminded that in the church, Jesus is Lord.

Jesus is Lord in the world. It makes all the difference in the world whether we are going out to help Christ *become* King in the world, or going out because Christ *is* King in the world. Whether we are trying to make Him King or whether we are witnessing to His Kingship will predetermine much of what we do and its effectiveness. The one approach makes evangelism and renewal an anxious, nervous, even angry activity; the other makes it a joyous, free, open, and grateful form of life and work. It will make a great difference whether we are seeking to rescue individual souls from the historical process, or seeking to testify to the Lordship of Christ over the process of history itself.

This is the way the New Testament looked upon Jesus, upon themselves, upon the church, and upon the world. Christ is God's radical demand upon us. He must be obeyed and with Him is the victory over the world. To obey and follow Him is not to avoid the cross but to find it. His victory, His glory, and the recognition by every tongue that He is Lord is the outcome of His sacrifice and of His call to men to live in the light of the cross.

This emphasis in no way minimizes the Saviorhood of the crucified Christ; rather it insists that that Saviorhood can only be realized in the light of His Lordship. It is to remind us of the words which were written on the cross in Hebrew, Greek, and Latin, so that any man anywhere could see and understand: "This is the King."

What's It All About? 3

THE ESSENCE OF EVANGELISM

John W. Alexander

The words *evangelism* and *evangelize* do not appear in the King James New Testament. The word *evangelist* or its plural form occurs three times: Acts 21:8 refers to a man who was an *evangelist;* II Timothy 4:5 is a charge *to do* the work of an *evangelist;* Ephesians 4:11 speaks of *evangelists,* those who, in distinction from others, have been endowed by God with special gifts.

In the Greek New Testament there are numerous occurrences of two significant words: *euangelion,* a noun meaning "good news, gospel," and *euangelizomai,* a verb meaning "to announce good news, to proclaim the gospel."

Therefore, I believe evangelism is the attempt to perform two services. The first is *to make known the message of the gospel* (communication, proclamation).

In evangelism we aim at another person's *mind* so that he may be informed about God and his relationship to Him, what God has done to improve that relationship, and what he must do to respond properly to God's action. If such communication is to be successful, two requirements must be met. Statements must be clear (Col. 4:4), and the statements must be heard and sufficiently understood. At this point we must be able to overcome the problem of outside interference, "minds blinded by the god of this passing age" (cf. II Cor. 3–4). Therefore our prayer must be that we receive adequate power from the Lord Himself (Col. 4:2-4).

The second service in evangelism is that of *seeking to bring about conversions.* We aim at a person's *will* so that he will act after he has received the information about his relationship to God. We persuade men (II Cor. 5:11) to act (Rom. 10:9-10). Thus, if we are to evangelize according to Scriptural directives, we need both a burning heart and a clear mind (Jer. 1:6-9).

Biblical evangelism must include both declaration and persuasion. Declaration without persuasion can be sterile and dead. It may be factually correct and informationally complete, but if all it does is communicate information—be it ever so clear—it is no more than instruction. A person who does only this, no matter how well he does it, may be a good instructor, but he is not an evangelist.

Nor is persuasion itself enough. Without proper declaration it can be dangerous. We may urge, cajole, and do everything in our power to persuade men to become Christians, but no matter how earnest our endeavors and fervent our efforts, if all we do is attempt to persuade, it is no more than exhortation. A person who only exhorts, no matter how eloquent, may be a mover of people, but he is not an evangelist.

If we are to do the work of evangelists, we must be active both in clearly communicating the gospel of Jesus Christ and in persuading men to respond to that message.

What is the message we endeavor to communicate? In a nutshell it is this: God has carried out His plan of redemption in sending His Son to save sinners. But to understand this, we need to know something about God, man, and Christ.

There is no rigid outline or blueprint for communicating these truths to a non-Christian. However, there are two basic categories of presentation into which the specific types fit, expository and topical.

The expository presentation takes a passage of Scripture and explains it to the person we are endeavoring to evangelize. In this instance the message is structured around the particular passage. A precedent for this type of message presented to a non-Christian is recorded in Acts 8:26-35.* Notice especially verse 35, "Then Philip . . . beginning with this scripture told him the good news of Jesus." Examples of other passages which Christians today find useful in expounding the good news of Jesus are: John 3:1-21; John 4:4-42; John 9:1-38.

*References are to the Revised Standard Version unless otherwise indicated.

The topical presentation uses a series of ideas based on Scripture. The message is structured around a series of themes, questions, or topics. A precedent for this type presented to non-Christians is recorded in Acts 17:16-34. Notice how Paul directs the line of thought to a specific confrontation between the listeners and the Lord Jesus Christ.

Below are two examples of different ways by which the content of the gospel can be arranged and presented topically.

Example 1

Christianity is Christ. Christianity is not a philosophy of life or a code of ethics, but a relationship to a living Person. The gospel is the good news of God's love for us shown in His saving activity in Jesus Christ. John tells us, "For God so loved the world that he gave his only Son" (John 3:16). And Paul declares, " . . . that Christ died for our sins in accordance with the scriptures, that he was buried, that he was raised on the third day . . . " (I Cor. 15:3, 4). Man's deep need and God's gracious provision in Christ constitute the theme of the gospel.

Since the good news concerns a Person, there is no set plan or formula to present it. We do not always describe a dear friend in the same way: color of his eyes, character, profession, hobbies, etc. Rather we begin with whatever is of interest and relevance at the moment. So in our witness of Jesus Christ we may begin at one time with His claims, at another His death, or another the particular way He can meet a human need. As we present the gospel we must realize that while there is only one way to God there are a hundred ways to Jesus Christ. Let us be flexible enough to present our Lord in all His varied richness.

The following brief outline presents the essentials of the gospel. There is something to be believed as well as Someone to be received. For each point there is a Scriptural reference statement in the words of Christ. To evangelize successfully, one must memorize key verses of Scripture and know where they are found. But remember: The following points are *not* necessarily to be used in this order, or all at once.

I. Jesus Christ

A. He is completely human; He knows what it is to be tired, thirsty, and sorrowful (John 4:6; 11:35).

B. Yet He is sinless and equal with God: "I always do what is pleasing to him" (John 8:29). "Which of you convicts me of sin?" (John 8:46). " . . . the Son of man has authority . . . to forgive sins" (Mark 2:10). "I and the Father are one" (John 10:30).

C. Other key Biblical statements are: "His name will be called Wonderful Counsellor, Mighty God, Everlasting Father, Prince of Peace" (Isa. 9:6). "In the beginning was the Word, and the Word was with God, and the Word was God" (John 1:1). "Though he was in the form of God [He] did not count equality with God a thing to be grasped" (Phil. 2:6).

II. Man's Need. The Bible describes man as being in revolt against his Creator; thus he is a sinner by nature and practice. He wants to be independent from God, to live as if God did not exist.

A. The human predicament is analyzed by Jesus Christ: "What comes out of a man is what defiles a man. For from within, out of the heart of a man, come evil thoughts . . . theft, murder, adultery, coveting . . . slander, pride . . . " (Mark 7:20-23). Man has evil thoughts, acts, attitudes, and words.

B. Other Biblical statements diagnose the disease of which the above are symptoms: "All we like sheep have gone astray" (Isa. 53:6). "Your iniquities have made a separation between you and your God" (59:2). "The heart is deceitful above all things and desperately corrupt" (Jer. 17:9). " . . . although they knew God they did not honor him as God or give thanks to him" (Rom. 1:21). " . . . all have sinned and fall short of the glory of God" (3:23).

III. God's Provision. God came to live among us in the Person of His Son. "God was in Christ reconciling the world to himself, not counting their trespasses against them" (II Cor. 5:19).

A. Jesus summed up His mission as a life of service and a death of sacrifice in these words: "For the Son of man also came not to be served but to serve, and to give his life as a ransom for many" (Mark 10:45). "This is my blood of the covenant, which is poured out for many for the forgiveness of sins" (Matt. 26:28).

B. The cross and resurrection are at the heart of the gospel: "He was wounded for our transgressions" (Isa. 53:5). "This Jesus God raised up, and of that we all are witnesses" (Acts 2:32).

C. The good news for us is: "But God shows his love for us in that while we were yet sinners Christ died for us" (Rom. 5:8). " . . . [He] was put to death for our trespasses and raised for our justification" (4:25). Paul affirms that Christ was raised: "He appeared to Cephas . . . the twelve . . . more than five hundred brethren at one time" (I Cor. 15:5, 6).

IV. God's Appeal. When a person hears the gospel, he is called to repent and believe. *In repentance I acknowledge my sin before God; in faith I commit myself to the Living Christ who is ready to become my Lord and Savior.*

A. Jesus began His preaching with the appeal, "repent, and believe in the gospel" (Mark 1:15). Paul summarized his appeal to both Jews and Greeks as, "repentance toward God and faith in our Lord Jesus" (Acts 20:21, NAS).

B. Faith is more than intellectual assent; it is trust in a person to whom we turn over our lives. "But to all who received him, who believed in his name, he gave power to become children of God" (John 1:12). Christianity is a personal relationship to Jesus Christ. The invitations of Christ emphasize this reality: "Come to me, all who labor and are heavy laden, and I will give you rest" (Matt. 11:28). "I am the bread of life; he who comes to me shall not hunger" (John 6:35). "I am the light of the world; he who follows me will not walk in darkness, but will have the light of life" (John 8:12). " . . . everyone who commits sin is a slave to sin . . . if the Son makes you free, you will be free indeed" (John 8:34, 36). " . . . I am the way, and the truth, and the life; no one comes to the Father, but by me" (John 14:6).

C. God wants us to be certain that we have eternal life: " . . . God gave us eternal life and this life is in his Son . . . I write this to you who believe in the name of the Son of God, that you may know that you have eternal life" (I John 5:11-13).

Example 2

As individuals men have the problems of loneliness, fear, no meaning, no purpose, despair, guilt, and so forth. Society experiences hatred, strife, oppression, theft, deceit, falsehood, adultery, gossip, murder, war, and so forth.
What's the Cause? What's the Cure? Let's begin with God:

I. God. There are two types of information we need to know:

A. What He *has done* (His deeds)

For example:

Genesis 1:1	Ephesians 2:1-10
Matthew 13:24-30, 36-43	Colossians 1:17

B. What He *is like* (His character, attributes)

For example:

Deuteronomy 32:4 & Galatians 6:7-8	Malachi 3:6
Leviticus 11:44	Mark 10:27
Psalm 103:8	John 4:24
Psalm 139:1-2	Ephesians 4:30
Psalm 139:7-10	Hebrews 1:10-12
Isaiah 46:9	I John 1:5
Isaiah 46:10-11	I John 4:16
Jeremiah 9:24	I John 5:19
Jeremiah 44:4 & Zechariah 8:16-17	

We cannot prove to a skeptic that God exists, but we can tell him what God is like and what He has done. "Good news" apart from God can end up being meaningless.

Beware the danger of superficial evangelism which fails to confront men with the living God. Do not fall for the temptation to press for decision before a man knows what the issues are. The first issue is that he must deal with God Himself.

II. Man

A. God, who made everything, made us to have fellowship with Himself and with one another (Mark 12:30-31).

B. Man rebelled and turned away from God (Isa. 53:6). The *consequences* of his rebellion are severe:

1. God suffers

2. Other people suffer from my attitudes and actions (Mark 7:21-23).

3. Man suffers in several ways. He faces: an inner void which needs to be filled, a moral disease which needs to be healed, a separation (from God) which needs to be bridged (Isa. 59:2). A penalty which needs to be paid (James 1:14, 15).

The *Cure?* Man is incapable of producing a cure. He is not good enough to fill his own void, to heal his own disease, to close the gap, or to escape the penalty (Rom. 3:20).

Conclusion at this point: The picture is dark and the outlook is bleak for him as an individual and for our society as a group.

III. Christ. Good news! God produced a remedial solution: God became a man in the person of Jesus Christ to solve those problems (Col. 1:19-20).

A. Jesus Christ lived a perfect life (I Peter 2:22).

He died as a substitute to pay our death penalty (Mark 10:45).

C. He returned from the dead (I Cor. 15:3-4).

D. He is alive today and offers us new life (John 10:10.) He can fill any void (John 6:35-37). He can heal my disease (Mark 3:17). He can bridge the gap to God (II Cor. 5:16, 21). He has paid my death penalty (I Peter 3:18).

IV. Man's Response.

A. He must admit that he is a rebel—a sinner (Rom. 3:23).

B. He must recognize that Jesus Christ is the only solution to his problem (John 14:6).

C. He must repent of his sin (Luke 13:5).

D. He must receive Jesus Christ (John 1:12).

V. Cost?

A. This solution cost God an enormous price (I Peter 1:18-19).

B. It costs a man nothing (Eph. 2:8-9).

C. It will cost him everything (Luke 9:23-24).

VI. Choice

A. There are only two choices (Rom. 6:23). The consequences are serious and the majority are making the wrong choice (Matt. 7:13-14).

B. Reasons for deciding to receive Christ.

  1. God will benefit.

  2. Others will benefit from my being a better citizen (Gal. 5:22-23).

  3. A man will benefit from the void filled, the disease healed, the gulf bridged, the penalty paid (John 3:16).

C. The decision must be made immediately (II Cor. 6:2).

Foundations
Are Important 4

BIBLICAL FOUNDATIONS OF EVANGELISM

Samuel H. Moffett

The task of evangelism is always before us, whether as individual Christians or as part of a congregation, and this is generally known both in our homeland and in lands overseas. We feel an urgency to meet the needs of man and to carry out the mandate given to us by our Lord and Master.

To clarify our task, we must ask, What is the gospel? Evangelism is evangelizing, preaching the gospel, the "evangel," with a power, with a purpose, and with a strategy. If therefore evangelism is preaching the evangel, what is the evangel?

We find the answer in part from word study. In Anglo-Saxon the equivalent of the Greek word *evangel* is *good spiel* or *gospel*. Notice how this word makes good common sense. *Gospel* has a nice, pious ring to it, but we forget that it probably means as little to the average man today as the Greek word *evangel* did to the Anglo-Saxons. Today's word is not *evangel*, not even *gospel;* for modern man the word is *good news.* It is a good lesson in evangelism to note that when the American Bible Society called its latest edition of the New Testament just that—*Good News for Modern Man*—it had a best seller. The evangel is the good news.

It is what the angel said at Bethlehem, "Do not be afraid; I have good news for you" (Luke 2:10, NEB). It is what Jesus preached in Galilee: "the good news of the kingdom of God" (Luke 8:1, NEB). It is what brought Paul unafraid before kings and governors to say, "I am not ashamed of the (good news)" (Rom. 1:16*).

*References are to the King James Version unless otherwise indicated.

38

There are three key Biblical proclamations of the good news: the *apostolic,* the *Messianic,* and the *angelic.* Any Biblical definition of the evangel must encompass all three.

I. The Apostolic Evangel. Paul said, "I am not ashamed of the gospel [the evangel, the good news]." But why wasn't he? He was a Roman, writing to Rome. Was not the gospel a ridiculous thing for a Roman to be preaching—full of nonsense about love, meekness, humility, and turning the other cheek, and about a god who died like a criminal? It was rubbish for slaves or women, not for world-conquering Romans. This was Rome's attitude—self-sufficient and powerful. Its standard was the eagle; its symbols the axe and the short sword. Not the cross. Rome wanted victory, not sacrifice; power, not meekness.

So Paul stood up and said to Rome, "The good news I have for you is *power.*" This is the first characteristic of the apostolic evangel. It is power. "I am not ashamed of the gospel, for it is the power of God unto salvation" (Rom. 1:16). As a creedal Calvinist with tendencies toward a propositional theology, I find that I often need this explosive reminder that there is a dynamic and a movement in the good news which will not suffer the compression and containment of any creed, however true. It is precisely because the evangel is, first of all, power, that evangelism, which is the proclaiming of the evangel, can never be equated with the cold, clear transmission of orthodoxy to the unbeliever.

This is not to minimize the indispensable nature of truth. But in the Bible, evangelism begins with power because the evangel *is* power. This happens not only with Paul in the Book of Romans. Consider also the significant sequence in the great commissioning scene which opens the Acts of the Apostles. How does Jesus train His first evangelists? First, says Luke, "he shewed himself alive" to them "by many infallible proofs" (Acts 1:3). But that was not enough. The "infallible proofs" did not make them evangelists. They knew they were still not prepared, and asked for more information. But Jesus rebuked them. "It is not for you to know" (1:7). Knowledge does not make evangelists, either. The evangel is not inside information about "times and seasons"; it is not "infallible proofs." It is power. Jesus said, "Ye shall receive power . . . and . . . be witnesses unto me" (1:8).

The power of the Spirit received, the power of a personal encounter with God, this is the good news of the evangel. So Paul, remembering a cataclysmic moment on the road to Damascus, says, "I am not ashamed of the good news, for it is the power of God unto salvation." The good news, however, is not always cataclysmic, for experiences will differ. With John Wesley at Aldersgate the experience was only "a warming of the heart." The good news is not the experience, but the power. The "good news of salvation," as William Barclay remarks in his commentary on that phrase in Ephesians 1:13, "is news of that power which wins us forgiveness from past sin, liberation from present sin, strength for the future to conquer sin. It is good news of victory" (Barclay, *Letters to the Galatians and Ephesians*).

This is heady stuff. It is as exciting as the taste of new wine. No old bottles will be able to contain it. I like and I preach the old words—*ransom, justification, satisfaction, reconciliation.* They are all true and Biblical. But they are essentially theological, and it can be as much of a mistake to confuse theology with evangelism as to mistake social service for evangelism. The word for the evangel, the word for today, is *power.* Not black power, or student power, or flower power; but God power. "I am not ashamed of the good news, for it is the power of God." The evangel is power.

Secondly, the evangel is *fact.* Having said emphatically that the evangel is power, I must add, and just as emphatically, that the evangel is also fact, and it is the business of theology to help us distinguish fact from fiction in the evangel. When the Reformation was being criticized for lack of saints' bones and wonder and miracles, John Calvin dryly remarked that Satan also had his miracles, "to delude the ignorant and inexperienced. Magicians and enchanters have always been famous for miracles," he observed (*Institutes,* Dedication, p. 4).

Evangelism may be power, and not theology, but the same apostle who was so excited about the power of the gospel, as he begins his letter to the Romans, goes on in the same epistle to write twelve of the most closely reasoned theological chapters in all of Scripture. Paul was the greatest evangelist in history not only because he had power, but because he had *learning.* So many charismatic movements fail at this point. They speak with the power of the Spirit, so they say. How strange that through them the Spirit does not speak any theology worth remembering.

Similarly, the "infallible proofs" do not make evangelists. It is true that power does. But if the evangelist's evangel is not true to the facts, it is not good news at all. It is only wishful thinking or false propaganda, which is even worse. A few months after the communists overran Peking, I heard of a slogan they had posted in huge characters across the walls of a bookstore in Tientsin. It was a warning, I suppose, against what they called "dangerous thoughts." The slogan was this: "Any fact which is not in accord with revolutionary theory is not a true fact." Without tongue in cheek, the Christian can say: "Any preaching which is not in accord with the facts is not the true evangel." "What the apostles preached," says James S. Stewart, "was neither a philosophy of life nor a theory of redemption. They preached events. They anchored their Gospel to history" (*Thine Is the Kingdom*, p. 29).

The classic apostolic capsule of the facts of the evangel is in I Corinthians 15. Here Paul writes: "Do you still hold fast the gospel as I preached it to you? . . . First and foremost, I handed on to you the facts . . . " (vs. 2, 3, NEB). The facts he chooses as his summary of the good news are the two most fundamental facts of all existence: death and life. In Christian symbolism they are portrayed by the cross and the crown. There is no evangel without both of these facts.

The first fact of the good news is *death*. There is this much at least to be said for Paul: he tells it like it is. Someone has remarked that he was truly called to be an ambassador, but he was no diplomat. He breaks all the rules of modern preaching and begins with the last things men want to hear about—*death*.

But where can we honestly begin in a world like ours? The one brutal fact of modern life is death. Some, like the secular existentialists, say that death is the only really meaningful fact, for life has lost its meaning. This is not true, but death is certainly an inescapable fact. The hand on the clock of the Atomic Scientists Bulletin—the hand that marks the death of the world, the nuclear holocaust, stands now at seven minutes to twelve, the closest the world has been to death, the scientists think, since 1953 (*Christianity Today*, Feb. 2, 1968, p. 31).

If the good news must begin with the facts, perhaps death is as good a fact as any with which to begin. It is a fact man had better learn to recognize and accept. But I must confess that there have been times when I thought Paul was a little too blunt about it. I have been tempted to play more lightly with the word *evangel*. I wanted to cry out that it means good news, not bad. I wanted to preach of the love of God, not of sin and death.

My intentions were good, and I was partly right. More right, I think, than those evangelists of doom who enjoy preaching about sin and death and all the fires of hell. D. L. Moody, a better evangelist than they, said, "Don't preach about hell if you can do it without tears." My heart was in the right place, but I was wrong if I thought I could leave death out of the gospel, for death is the first fact of the good news, says Paul.

But where is the good news in death? Gilbert K. Chesterton tells of standing on the Mount of Olives with Father Waggett, looking down at Calvary. "Well, anyhow," said the priest unexpectedly, "it must be obvious to anybody that the doctrine of the Fall is the only cheerful view of human life." Chesterton was startled for a moment, until he reflected that it is the only cheerful view because it is the only profound view (quoted, H. C. Alleman, *The Christian Century*, Dec. 29, 1943, p. 153).

But there is even more cheer than that in the evangel's "fact of death." The first fact of the gospel, as Paul sums it up in I Corinthians 15 is: Christ's death, not the sinner's. Or, as that remarkably durable Puritan, John Owen, put it three hundred years ago: the good news is "the death of death in the death of Christ" (*The Death of Death*).

The good news is that the hard facts of sin and death are never isolated in the Biblical evangel apart from the love of God, and the deepest proof of that love is "that while we were yet sinners, Christ died for us" (Rom. 5:8). The Bible does not dodge the fact that sin causes death. "The wages of sin is death" (Rom. 6:23). But its spotlight is not on man's death by sin, but on Christ's death for sin. That is the good news.

If this be so, the evangelist can never be vindictive. He must present the facts without apology, but also in love, without condemnation. Paul Little tells how a drunk bumped into Charles Trumbull on the train. He was "spewing profanity and filth" (*How to Give Away Your Faith*, p. 43). He lurched into the seat beside Trumbull and offered him a swallow from his flask. Trumbull started to shrink back. A lesser man might have blasted the man for his sin and condition, but instead Trumbull politely declined the drink and said, "No thank you, but I can see you are a generous man." The man's eyes lit up, and it was the beginning of a conversation that brought the man to the Savior. That is evangelism. It communicates the good news which is not condemnation but salvation. Up against the hard facts of sin and death, it places another fact: that "God sent the Son into the world, not to condemn the world, but that the world might be saved through him" (John 3:17, RSV).

The second and greatest fact of the good news is *life*. Christ, who died for our sins was raised to "life." The first fact is the cross. The second fact is the empty tomb and the crown of life. Let us make sure our evangel contains both facts. "To preach only the atonement, the death apart from the life," says P. T. Forsyth, "or only the person of Christ, the life apart from the death . . . is all equally one-sided and extreme to [the point of] falsity" (*The Cruciality of the Cross*, p. 42).

There is more than a careful balance between these two facts in the gospel. There is also movement. The dynamic of the gospel is its movement from death to life. The Bible calls this *salvation*.

It should be noted that this movement is a reversal of man's normal understanding of history. The natural, mournful rhythm of existence as history records it is that man lives, and then he dies. Christian history joyfully turns this around: we were dead, but now we have come alive. For "God, rich in mercy, for the great love he bore us, brought us to life with Christ even when we were dead in our sins; it is by his grace you are saved" (Eph. 2:4, NEB).

We often laugh at the line, "Brother, are you saved?" We hear it as an evangelistic cliché; but in a world where more and more people confess that they have somehow lost all sense of meaning in their lives, what more central question is there than "Brother, are you really alive?" This is what *saved* means. The good news is life: we have moved from death to life.

But as always in the evangel, the accent is on Christ. As only Christ's death makes good news of death, so only as Christ "was raised to life" do we have life. It took a miracle to wrench the course of history from its grim life-to-death sequence, and bring it back again from death to life. It took a miracle, the miracle on which history hinges—the resurrection. Death is the first fact, but not the greatest fact. Not even the cross stands as the hinge. "No cross, no crown," said William Penn, for without the cross the gospel is a frothy thing. But Paul suggests "no crown, no gospel." He says, "If Christ was not raised, then our gospel is null and void, and so is your faith" (I Cor. 15:14, NEB).

The new breed of theologians has been right at one point, at least. Without the resurrection, God is quite dead. But what they have not been so willing to recognize is that without God, man is just as dead. Without Him, life loses its meaning. Then it loses itself. This is precisely how Malcolm Muggeridge, the acid-tongued social critic of our times, describes the world of the imminent future: "psychiatric wards bursting at the seams," and "the suicide rate up to Scandinavian proportions," as we rise "on the plastic wings of *Playboy* magazines" (*Christianity Today,* Feb. 2, 1969, p. 54).

D. T. Niles describes the situation this way: "There are . . . attempts to make life meaningful apart from God. Existentialism is only the best known of these attempts. The Gospel answers that true meaning lies in the fact that we are the sons of God. There are attempts," he continues, "to direct man's struggle for food away from man's hunger for God. Communism is only the best known of these attempts. The Gospel answers, living is not Life, for Life is to live with God" (*That They May Have Life,* p. 39). The "good news of salvation" is life.

This, then, is the apostolic evangel: power, and death, and life. There is no evangelism without the fire, without the cross, and without the crown.

II. The Messianic Evangel. But even earlier than the evangelism of the apostles came Jesus' own evangelistic ministry. There is a direct relationship between the two, of course. They "proclaimed" what He "did": their good news was His power, His death, His resurrection. But there is also a significant difference. Jesus' own evangel as He preached it in the villages of Galilee focused on a part of the gospel which not all evangelists have recognized. What Jesus preached was the evangel of the kingdom. And that is, in a sense, a social gospel. It is a prophetic gospel.

Perhaps we have not recognized it as the gospel because we have not wanted to do so. We complain that it confuses the issue. It seems to take the cutting edge, the call for personal decision, from evangelism. We fear that it dilutes the spirit with politics. But kings are inescapably political, and Jesus is King!

What are we to do with Jesus' *evangel of the kingdom?* What He preached was more than personal salvation. The gospel of His kingdom is "peace, integrity, community, harmony and justice," as J. Hoekendijk so rightly declares (*The Church Inside Out,* p. 21). For the kingdom of God is what the King came to establish, and He is "Prince of Peace" (Isa. 9:6) and the "king [that] shall reign in righteousness" (Isa. 32:1). All this may be social gospel, but it is no heresy. It is simply the affirmation of the lordship of Jesus Christ. It is as old as the oldest creed of the church, and it was the first gospel preached by the Lord of the church, as recorded by Luke: "The Spirit of the Lord is upon me, because he has anointed me to preach good news to the poor. He has sent me to proclaim release to the captives and recovering of sight to the blind, to set at liberty those who are oppressed, to proclaim the acceptable year of the Lord" (Luke 4:18, 19, RSV).

The earliest creed of the church, Bible theologians tell us, was, "Jesus is Lord." This was an even older test of orthodoxy, apparently, than the beloved evangelistic companion phrase, "Jesus is Savior." Paul used it as just such a test. "No man can say that Jesus is the Lord," he wrote to the Corinthians, "except by the Holy Ghost" (I Cor. 12:3).

But once again let me run up the warning flag against separating the two statements. The Bible does not give us one creed for pious evangelists, "Jesus is Savior," and another creed for broad-minded activists, "Jesus is Lord." The creed of the church and the teaching of Scripture is that "Jesus is Lord and Savior," and let not man put asunder what God has joined together. Joining the two reminds the evangelist that the broad ethics of the kingdom are an essential part of the gospel. Bringing the two together reminds the activist that the boundaries of the kingdom are not the boundaries of this world, that the kingdom comes not by social reform but by the will of God, and that men are called not to establish the kingdom, but to enter it. "Christ's ethical teachings are the righteousness of that Kingdom," writes John Bright. "As such, of course, they are incumbent upon all the servants of the Kingdom. But by the same token they lie beyond men who do not acknowledge its lordship. . . . To realize the ethics of the Kingdom it is first necessary that men submit to the rule of that Kingdom" (*The Kingdom of God,* p. 221f.). John Calvin said the same thing, echoing the words of his Lord: "No one can enter the Kingdom of heaven except he who has been regenerated" (*Instruction in Faith,* Fuhrmann tr., p. 42 f., quoting John 3:3).

In other words, no one can say, "Jesus is Lord," who has not first said, "Jesus is Savior." The Messianic evangel calls for commitment both to Christ's person and to His program.

III. The Angelic Evangel. Earliest of all the evangels in the New Testament, earlier than the apostolic evangel and earlier than the Messianic, was the evangel of the angels. It is also the least complicated. The angels sang with joy: "Do not be afraid; I have good news for you: there is great joy coming to the whole people.

Today in the city of David a deliverer has been born to you—the Messiah, the Lord" (Luke 2:10, NEB).

The lost note in most of our evangelism is hilarity. The evangel is a theme for singing, and if we cannot sing it, it is not the gospel. It can be power and fact and ethics and invitation and all the rest, but take joy out of it, and it does not really grip the heart.

And we? We take this lovely, fragile, hilarious, singable thing, the gospel, and argue it. Or we take this simple thing, the good news, and make philosophy of it. Some years ago a distinguished professor came to Korea. He wanted to preach, so Graham Lee, one of the early missionary-evangelists, took him out to a little country church and prepared to interpret for him. The man's opening sentence was, "All thought is divided into two categories, the concrete and the abstract." Graham Lee took one look at that little country congregation of toothless grandmothers, sturdy farmers, and little children sitting on the bare, dirt floor, and instantly translated it, "I have come here all the way from America to tell you about the Lord Jesus Christ." And from that point on the sermon was firmly in the hands of the angels!

It is as simple as that—the gospel. If you cannot preach it, at least sing it. Proclaim it as truly and simply and as earnestly as you can. This world of ours is dying for the kind of happiness which the good news of the love of God in Christ has the power to give.

In the light of the Biblical foundation, who then is an evangelist, a teller of the good news? History has many examples of the true gospeler. Is he a Jonathan Edwards? a John Wesley? a Billy Sunday? a Whitefield? a Torrey? a Moody? Or does he minister in other more modern ways for our day, as a Billy Graham or kindred spirits? Are pastors not also evangelists as they carry out the Pauline exhortation: "do the work of an evangelist, make full proof of thy ministry" (II Tim. 4:5)? The church needs all kinds of evangelists, and generally has them. All Christians are in this category if they heed the Word of God and sense the Biblical basis for evangelism.

Those who obey discover a secret: we are not really the evangelists after all. *God is.* The Great Evangelist is with us, and in us, and for us. Our task is to open the door a little so that men can go in and find Him. That was how Sam Shoemaker saw it, as quoted in his wife's tribute:

I Stand by the Door

"I stand by the door," he wrote.
"I neither go too far in, nor stay too far out.
The door is the most important door in the world—
It is the door through which men walk when they find God.
Men die outside that door, as starving beggars die
On cold nights, in cruel cities, in the dead of Winter—
Nothing else matters compared to helping them find it,
And open it, and walk in, and find Him . . .
So I stand by the door . . .
You can go in too deeply and stay in too long,
And forget the people outside the door.
As for me, I shall take my old accustomed place,
Near enough to God to hear Him, and know He is there,
But not so far from men as not to hear them,
And remember they are there, too.
Where? Outside the door—
Thousands of them, millions of them.
But—more important for me—
One of them, two of them, ten of them,
Whose hands I am intended to put on the latch.
So I shall stand by the door and wait
For those who seek it.
'I had rather be a door-keeper . . . '
So I stand by the door."

You can't be an evangelist, you say? "All right," says God. "I'll settle for that. Just be a doorkeeper. I'll be the evangelist." Will you settle for that?

Preacher, Do Your Part 5

THE PASTOR-PREACHER IN EVANGELISM

Harold J. Ockenga

Evangelism is one of many facets in pastoral work, yet it must be ranked as the most important. We must remember that the ascended and glorified Lord gave gifts unto men. He gave some men gifts to be apostles, some to be prophets, some to be evangelists, and some to be pastors and teachers (Eph. 4:11). These different gifts overlap. A pastor is shepherd of the flock, teacher of truth, minister to human needs, comforter to the brokenhearted and troubled, administrator of local church affairs, and preacher of the truth.

Paul joined the gift of pastor and teacher, for a pastor must both preach the truth and teach his people. As preacher, he proclaims the truth, he challenges people to make decisions, and he leads them to faith in Christ. This may not be the office of an evangelist, but it is the work of an evangelist when it is done by the pastor.

Certain prerequisites exist for the pastor as evangelist. Certainly he needs those prerequisites in the other aspects of the work of the ministry, but they are of paramount importance in reference to evangelism. First he must be a man of convictions.

The pastor-evangelist must have convictions concerning the Bible. He must have a high view of inspiration, holding to the Word of God as absolute truth. Such a view is quite different from that of the liberal who regards the Bible as merely the record of a

48

developing religious consciousness in the Hebrew people, a perspective based upon naturalism as a philosophy and evolution as a methodology. For him the Bible becomes a record of the natural religious development of the Hebrew people from polytheism to henotheism to monotheism, and finally to ethical monotheism. The books of the Bible are rearranged and re-dated so that the content of the Bible harmonizes with such presupposition. For him the Bible is not God's revelation, but rather a record of man's search for and finding of God. For the liberal, Jesus was a man who had a unique consciousness of sonship with God. He was a moral teacher whose example we may follow in order to find God as He found God, through prayer, sacrifice, loving service, self-denial, and obedience. For him the atonement through the crucifixion and bodily resurrection of Christ is merely a theoretical form of a permanent truth, namely, the love of God. To the liberal, the gospel is a message of filial piety, of brotherhood, of social understanding, and of human betterment. Such a view prevents a pastor from being an evangelist.

The pastor-evangelist must also hold a different view from that of the neo-orthodox theologian. Neo-orthodoxy speaks of truth and of revelation, but it fails to identify it with the written Word of God. For the neo-orthodox theologian the Bible is the region or framework in which God speaks. If he is to hear God speak through a personal encounter, it must be in the framework of the Bible, but the Bible itself is not that spoken Word. Because of this disassociation of revelation from the Bible, the neo-orthodox theologian is not concerned about the scientific, geographic, or historical accuracy of the Bible. He only uses it as the means by which the truth is made known to him through encounter. This approach also leaves the pastor-evangelist without an evangelistic message.

The pastor as an evangelist must have the conviction that the Bible is the infallible Word of God written; that it is inspired throughout, trustworthy, authentic, truthful, and inerrant. As the Word of God written, it may be quickened by the Holy Spirit to become the means of enlightenment and salvation to the individual. Nevertheless, it *is* true, whether or not the individual is quickened, whether he heeds or rejects the Word. This gives a sense of certainty to the pastor in his evangelistic message.

The pastor as an evangelist must have a conviction concerning theology. We live in a day when theology is disparaged and when the great theological systems are considered antiquated. Theology forms the bones, the structure of a sermon; without it a sermon is a mere glob or mass. That theological framework may be Calvinism, Augustinianism, or Arminianism, but the preacher must be unafraid of being committed to a theology. Such a commitment will guard him from moving off onto tangents of his own.

The pastor must be a man of convictions in reference to truth. There is much talk today about an experience or a fact being true to the individual who believes it, but not necessarily being true objectively. This is sheer nonsense. A fact is either true, or it is false. The laws of contradiction must be applied to all statements of the truth. Truth must be self-consistent. It must conform to reality. The preacher must not be afraid of antitheses; he must be able to say, "This is not that." He must distinguish between what is true and what is false. All this is quite opposed to the modern Hegelian synthetic method which is able to absorb everything as part of the sum-total of truth.

Another way of speaking of this is to require the absolute nature of truth over against relativism. Relativism has invaded physics, history, and ethics, but it must be resisted in the area of truth, or there can be no evangelistic emphasis. We hold that the Bible is true, whether it is applied to an individual or not. Based on this premise, we believe that the doctrines taught in the Bible are also true.

A second prerequisite for the pastor as an evangelist is that he must be a man of spiritual experience. He needs the assurance which comes from knowledge of salvation. What contributes to his spiritual experience? Probably it will include Christian parents and a Christian home environment, church training through the Sunday school and related organizations, conversion which possibly occurred in an evangelistic service, peer influence in groups such as Christian Endeavor, Young Life, or Inter-Varsity Christian Fellowship, and service in which he tried and proved God's promises concerning prayer, trust, and works. All of these contribute to a rich spiritual experience.

A man of such experience can apply the evangelistic formulas which he knows will work. One such formula pertains to knowing Christ as Saviour. A careful analysis of New Testament preaching reveals that this involves *repentance,* or a change of mind concerning the importance of faith in Christ, *confession* of one's sinfulness and need of Christ as Savior, *turning* from one's own way to God's appointed way, and *commitment* to Christ as God's appointed mediator between Him and man. The emphasis upon these elements of salvation will give the pastor authority in leading souls to Christ.

A methodology exists also for the Spirit-filled life. Here the requirements are somewhat different. Confession comes first because it is necessary to admit that one is not living the spiritual life and needs to be filled with the Holy Spirit. The evidences of that may be found in his lack of the fruit of the Spirit, his failure to exercise a gift of the Spirit and the absence of the assurance of the Holy Spirit. Following confession comes complete and full consecration, whether it is called surrender, yieldedness, or consecration. Everything must be placed upon the altar as a prerequisite of the Spirit-filled life. With consecration must be prayer asking for the fulness of the Spirit (Luke 11:13), faith which believes God's promises (Heb. 3:7–4:11), and, finally, obedience to the will of God (Acts 5:32).

The pastor-evangelist must be engaged in prevailing prayer. This involves a condition of righteousness (James 5:16), prayer in the name of Christ (John 16:24; 14:15), prayer in the Spirit (Eph. 2:18; Rom. 8:26), prayer of agreement (Matt. 20:22), prayer of faith (Mark 11:24; James 5:16), prayer of committal (Ps. 37:5), and prayer of persistence (Luke 18:1; 11:8).

The formula for revival consists of a united confessing, united believing, united praying, and united witnessing. In like manner, conditions of a formula for blessing upon the local church consist of an emphasis upon world missions, local evangelism, Christian education, and humanitarian action. The pastor who acts within the framework of these formulas or methodologies will find an evangelistic witness which he could gain in no other way.

His spiritual experience must include the appropriation of the reality of the Holy Spirit's presence in his life. He must know the regenerating power of the Holy Spirit, the filling of the Holy Spirit, and the unction of the Holy Spirit. Just as Jesus was anointed by God the Father, and went about doing good, and could declare, "the Spirit of the Lord is upon me because he has anointed me to preach the good news . . . " (Luke 4:18, RSV), so John tells us that we as Christians "have been anointed by the Holy One" (I John 2:20, RSV). It is this functioning of the Holy Spirit as the Presence of God in the preacher which enables him to evangelize effectively.

Yet another prerequisite of a pastor as evangelist is a knowledge of the Scriptural answers to human needs. The sense of need arises from anxiety, fear, loneliness, guilt, insecurity, condemnation, weakness, reticence, and other failures of the spirit. It is only by a saturation in Scripture whereby he learns how God met the needs of Biblical personages who passed through similar experiences that he can gain the answers to meet the needs of these days.

I. The Evangelistic Emphasis in Preaching. In most common usage the two adjectives *evangelical* and *evangelistic* have decidedly different connotations. The word *evangelical* is most frequently used in reference to orthodox theology, whereas the word *evangelistic* describes the proclamation of the gospel with the goal of decisions for Christ. The Greek word *euangelidzo* means "to publish the good news." The content of that good news is the gospel, and the intent in proclaiming it is to bring people to an acceptance of it.

Jesus said, "I will make you fishers of men." If we are fishermen, then we need a hook for catching fish. That hook should be in every sermon. It consists of the content of the gospel. The emphasis must be upon the sinfulness of man and his inability to save himself. Men must be aware of falling short of the glory of God, of the fact that they have transgressed God's law and have violated their own consciences; they must learn that no man is able to justify himself in the sight of God. Over against this, we must proclaim the atonement made by our Lord Jesus Christ through His crucifixion and resurrection. God made Him to be sin for us, He who knew no sin, that through Him we might be made the righteousness of God. Our sins were laid upon Him. Our guilt was imputed to Him, and His righteousness, through perfect obedience to the will of God and through resurrection from the dead, is imputed to us. Sinful men need to recognize that they can be forgiven and accepted as holy in the sight of God. Along with these two important facts, we must emphasize the necessity for a personal commitment to faith in Jesus Christ. This gospel should be preached in all types of sermons and in every sermon. Whether a sermon is expository, doctrinal, biographical, textual, topical, polemic, or experiential, it should contain a simple statement of the gospel so that whoever hears will be confronted by Christ and His claims, and be compelled to make a decision. Every sermon should be constructed with this in mind, for it is the primary responsibility of the preacher.

The handling of the great doctrines of Scripture should be calculated to convince, to convert, and to bring men to an open confession of Christ. A master of this type of preaching was Clarence Edward Macartney. His great series of sermons on the doctrines of Scripture contained, in every message, a challenge to believe, to be converted, and to confess Christ. One can see how easily this is to be done in treating the Trinity, of which Christ is the executor of divine redemption, or in considering the deity of Christ, in which His sovereign claims rest upon us. Such a call can be included in a sermon that concerns the baptism of the Holy Spirit, the instrument of our regeneration and sanctification, or in a sermon about predestination, whereby the divine purposes are fulfilled. Sermons about repentance, our response to the gospel; contrition, which is an honest self-evaluation under the light of the gospel; adoption, which gives us standing in the family of God; or justification, whereby we are declared righteous in the sight of God, should also contain an evangelistic element. Doctrinal preaching such as this can include the major thrust of evangelism.

Preaching must be prepared and performed with the intention of homing in on a decision by the hearer. The conclusion should be prepared at the beginning, and the whole sermon should be developed with the conclusion in mind. Pastor-evangelists must ask: What am I driving at? What am I seeking to accomplish? What decision do I desire from the hearer? When these questions have been answered, everything in the sermon will point toward that objective.

II. The Evangelistic Methods of a Pastor. A pastor should make use of to a large variety of methods in his evangelism. One of the most prominent and well-tried methods is that of preaching missions, sometimes called revivals (although legitimately, no man can call a series of meetings a revival until God has initiated the work of revival). Preaching missions are concentrated efforts on proclaiming the truth of salvation and in reaping a harvest. They involve the united effort of a congregation or a group of congregations. What individuals cannot do singly can be accomplished by united effort. This includes advertising through public media, personal contact by individuals, and special series of services in which preaching piles up the truth of Christianity and builds conviction in the minds and hearts of the hearers. Preaching missions should give individuals opportunity for making decisions and should confront the community with the claims of Christ regarding personal life and social relationships.

A preaching mission can be particularly influential through the powerful influence of a new voice. The same message which has been given by the pastor may be underscored in a different way by a different personality. It reinforces the truth which the pastor has been preaching and it strengthens the pastor's ministry. This provides for the possibility of revival quickening in the local congregation. Time and again a visiting preacher, possibly another pastor, has brought new life, reformation, and revival to a congregation.

Preaching missions should meet the problems of the day: indifference, opposition, a climate of unbelief, and the attitude that the gospel and Christ are irrelevant to the age in which we live.

If preaching is to be evangelistic, it must present the challenge of decision to people. Every sermon should lead to some desirable action; therefore, the preacher must be clear in what he asks the people to believe or do. True evangelism means challenging men to accept Christ as Savior and to confess Him as Lord before their fellowmen. There are many ways of doing this: the altar call, open confession, the inquiry room, after-meetings, the signing of cards, and uniting with the church. An important point to remember is that the methods must be adapted to the people who are expected to respond. The challenge must be to believers to consecrate all to Jesus Christ, to crucify the old man, and to unite with Christ in resurrection life and power. This results in the sanctification of individual lives.

Pastors must also challenge listeners to enter Christian service. A sense of vocation ought to be imparted to every kind of work a Christian does; and yet, there are some who are to go into specialized services of the church such as the ministry of preaching, of missions, of teaching, or of humanitarian service.

A good evangelistic pastor will practice a variety of methods and not single out merely one. For example, he will use personal visitation whereby he and members of his congregation call upon people for the purpose of a decision for Christ. The Coral Ridge Presbyterian Church with Pastor James D. Kennedy has been built upon this principle. Campus Crusade for Christ has grown in influence and fruitfulness through its emphasis upon visitation. It can be practiced in any congregation or community.

Radio is available for many churches. Through radio the evangelistic preaching may reach the sick, the confined, the travelers, those occupied with responsible duties and those shut in behind closed doors who otherwise do not want to be involved in church work. Radio has been, and will continue to be, one of the most fruitful means of evangelism.

Of course, not all churches will be able to afford television coverage of its services, or even a special television program. This avenue must not be neglected, however. Many television stations are willing to accept on a sustaining-time basis a program which is challenging to people and which meets their needs. One Boston station allowed me ten years of weekly television services on a sustaining-time basis for a program entitled, "I Want an Answer," which combined preaching and answering live questions called in at the time of the telecast.

The Sunday school has the largest field of evangelism at hand. Most churches begin their expansion and growth through the Sunday school. Every Sunday school should have a Decision Day at least once a year, the time when members of that Sunday school are brought face to face with the claims of Christ. Through the Sunday school, parents, friends, and neighbors can be approached.

Another method of evangelism which has proved effective throughout the years is literature in the form of books, articles, tracts, and texts. Admiral Coligny, the leader of the Huguenots, was converted through a tract. Anyone can pass out a tract. During my pastorate in Boston, one of the famous doctors of the city spent his Sunday afternoons passing out tracts in telephone booths, railroad stations, the airport, and on the Boston Common. He was most effective and fruitful in this work.

Large congregations, or those where members are widely scattered geographically, may find it effective to form small group gatherings to which unchurched neighbors are invited for the purpose of confronting them with the gospel. These small groups have mushroomed throughout America and hold promise of a quickening of the church.

Another valuable means of communication is the use of regional evangelistic conferences to study various methods and to stimulate and motivate evangelistic action. Preachers can and should learn from one another, and laymen need the impetus and stimulus of evangelistic pastors.

Both laymen and pastors can effectively use the lecture platform and prayer meetings in the streets, the methods Frances E. Willard so ably used to conquer the liquor traffic. The Salvation

Army has used them for reaching down-and-outers. I have used them on the Boston Common to confront thousands of people with the claims of Christ.

Youth meetings in the form of Youth for Christ, Teen Challenge, Youthtime, Inter-Varsity, Campus Crusade, and others have an evangelistic emphasis and should have a place in the program of the local pastor.

III. **Evangelistic Fruitfulness of Pastors.** Wherever and whenever there is an emphasis on evangelism, there is evidence of church growth. Some churches, however, grow at a very rapid rate and reach great numbers. Pastors should ask why this is so. The Institute of Church Growth at Fuller Theological Seminary analyzes the differences between mission fields where the gospel reaches only a few, and others where many are reached. This investigation and inquiry has resulted in remarkable church growth where evangelists have instituted usable methods. The same process of analysis should be true with the local congregation. When a church is experiencing great growth, it seems that we ought to ask questions which will reveal to us the reasons for such growth so that our evangelism is most fruitful.

Recent denominational growth and new movements should indicate to us that the day of evangelism has not passed. The methods used by the Pentecostals in Latin America certainly can be used by other groups in all branches of the church for the purpose of growth. This growth through conversions, changed lives, and consecration to lives of service produces joy and exultation in the congregations experiencing it. Such evangelistic emphasis contributes more to the spiritual life of God's people than any other activity. Where such life is exhibited, people are loyal to their congregation. They may move from one section of a city to another, but they remain faithful to their local congregation because of its program and emphasis.

Evangelism will carry the whole program of the church when it is emphasized. World missions is evangelism carried on abroad and should not be distinguished from evangelism at home. Similarly, the program of soul-winning carries Christian education and social action. If we as pastors keep alive the commission to go, make disciples, baptize them, and teach them all things which the Lord has commanded, we can be certain that the work of local congregations will prosper. Evangelism in the local church under the leadership of the pastor will turn the tide of decreasing influence and usher in a day of new power and effectiveness.

Let's March Abreast 6

THE CONGREGATION IN EVANGELISM

George E. Sweazey

The congregation is God's intended evangelistic agency. That is why He put the church on earth. Most of those who through the years have been brought into the Christian life have come in across the growing edge of a local church. Each church is a mission station surrounded by people who are missing what God sent His Son to earth to give them.

Most church members know this well enough. When Christians see the spiritual needs of those without Christ they zealously want to do something to help them to know the wonders of the new life in Jesus Christ. Unfortunately, most church members do not know what to do about it. In any meeting where evangelism is discussed, they will talk endlessly about the sort of evangelism they do not believe in. But if the chairman says, "Let's talk about what we can be doing," a great silence falls upon the room. This chapter will deal specifically with what can be done—that which is spiritually valid and possible in any church. "For you hold in your hands the very word of life" (Phil. 2:16, Phillips).

The Committee

Evangelism is the church's most urgent, but, unfortunately, sometimes its least pressing, task. It can always be postponed. A minister is never finished in his work with those already in the

58

church. Attending to the Lord's "other sheep that are not of this fold" is easily put off until some "free time" becomes available—a time that never seems to come. Lay workers, too, are under unremitting pressure to complete the tasks immediately at hand— preparing for the canvass, getting teachers for the church school, and so forth. Doing something about evangelism is postponed from month to month, from year to year, even from decade to decade. Because evangelism can be so easily neglected, the work must be anchored firmly within the structure of a congregation by the appointment of a committee that will submit regular reports to the church board. Then something is likely to happen.

A layman should be chairman of this committee. The minister may well be the coach of the evangelism team, but it will function best with a lay captain. A lay enthusiast will usually push the minister and everybody else. The committee may be a very few persons in a small church, or up to thirty members in a large one. It should have enough members to be in contact with most of the church organizations and activities. *Evangelism is not a special activity for special people at special times; it is a normal activity for all church people all the time.* Whether it is realized or not, every activity of the church can be directed in such a way that will help to reach the goals of an evangelism program.

Remember this, for it is of great importance: *No one person is the evangelist.* The evangelist is not the special speaker at mass meetings, or the warm-hearted Christian who asks about your soul, or the pastor of the church. Every person in the whole Christian fellowship, should be an evangelist. In the fourth century, Jerome said, "Baptism ordains the laity." When the layman was baptized, he was ordained to evangelize. If his church does not show him how to do it and give him opportunities, it has cheated him of a function God demands of him.

Seeing evangelism as the work of the whole church helps avoid the old suspicion of arrogance—"You ought to be like I am," or the manipulation—"Do what I say and you'll get right." Evangelism is not one person working on another person; it is God working through the fellowship on each person involved in it. The plea of evangelists is simply, "Come where these great things are happening!"

This chapter will show that evangelism encompasses a wide range of activities that take a great deal of time. For two thousand years Christians have been searching for a quick and easy method of evangelism. It will never be found. Nothing so great can be simple. But when the whole church is the evangelist, no one has too much to do. The evangelism committee can help provide opportunities for each member to contribute to the program.

Let us think of the committee at its first meeting. Imagine that it is trying to get a program of evangelism started in its church. Its first concern must be the congregation. All members are needed to make contacts with people outside the church, to draw newcomers into church participation, to reveal the beauty of the Christian faith, and to help new members get a sound start in the church and in Christian living. It can be assumed at the beginning that many members will have small interest in this. They may recoil from the word *evangelism;* they may shun interference with other people's religion, or lack of it; they may not want to "spoil a fine congregation" by bringing in strangers who might not be congenial. These attitudes are not consistent with Christianity, so they must be erased. Members can develop an eagerness to bring people into the church. It comes from gratitude, faith that is worth sharing, a deep concern for people, and the habit of looking for people to reach. These new attitudes must be laid upon the hearts of the church people in sermons, prayers, classes, and group discussions. The alert committee tries to plan for this.

The committee needs to determine clearly what it hopes will happen to people. What sort of person should evangelism try to produce? Is the goal to make "nice people"? To aim souls toward heaven? To radicalize people and separate them from an exploitive culture? Bringing people into a saving relationship with Jesus Christ may do everything necessary. "If anyone is in Christ, he is a new creation" (II Cor. 5:17*). The committee might describe a person in Christ as a person

(1) Who believes that God sent Christ to live, and teach, and die, and rise again to reveal His saving love for man. This truth will be the organizing center of that one's cosmology, anthropology, philosophy, and politics. It will illuminate his understanding of himself every minute of the day.

(2) Who has Jesus Christ, not just as a one-time Savior, but as an always-present friend and helper.

(3) Whose life is so dominated by love for God and people that

*References are to the Revised Standard Version unless otherwise indicated.

he is joyfully open to others of all sorts, ready to listen, to trust, to care, and to share their joy and sorrow. This will affect relationships at home and at work, in every social contact.

(4) Who is blazingly intolerant of all that blights and corrupts human life, of misery and injustice, and is therefore dedicated to the struggle against these by every means God gives.

(5) Who is eagerly learning more of God's truth from the Bible and the history of Christian experience.

(6) Whose conduct is governed by the love of Christ.

(7) Who is a consistent, growing, and strength-giving member of the church.

Without such a well-defined goal as a measure and guide for an evangelism program, its total "product" can too easily become the mumbling of some misunderstood responses and a new card in the church member file. We must realize that the great result can be only God's doing, but He commands His church to provide the circumstances. The committee has to ask whether the essential thing will be happening to those the church attracts. Will it happen in church services, or classes, or conversations, or by reading? Will it be radiated through the fellowship or caught from Christian friends? Will it perhaps come through joining in some effort to help people? A transformation of the church program might come from asking such questions. However, if a church is not organized to reveal Christ to newcomers, it will be no more than a religious racket for the members it already has.

The File of Prospective Members

Evangelistic invitations cannot be addressed, "To whom it may concern." There is no such person. Of the many needy people near your church, the only ones it will reach are those you have identified by name and face. The listing of these is the start of all evangelism. There are only four pieces of furniture that a church really needs. It can do without hymnals and pews, but it must have a Bible, a Communion table, furnishings for baptism, and a file of prospective members. That last is no anticlimax. The whole evangelistic field of the church should be in that file. Rarely will anyone be won whose name has not been listed there. The amount of evangelism will depend on how well that list is kept up. It will have four sections: "Not Yet Seen"; "For Cultivation"; "For Decision"; "Very Difficult."

The list is built by hard work from many sources:

(1) *Church school parents.* Many who think the church has nothing for them will, nevertheless, send their children. These people can be drawn closer through church school P.T.A. activities. Also, a church school enlargement program may well have parents in mind.

(2) *Visitors to church services.* In a small church, alert officers can get their names. A large church has to ask all attenders to register in order to get the names of visitors. Those who greet at the door can get addresses by asking, "May we send you news about the church?"

(3) *Participants in church activities.* Church clubs and classes try hard to attract outsiders as a first stage in evangelism. Their members are urged to bring new people. Special programs are planned for this purpose. Fishers of men use bait. A club for young married people has special evangelistic opportunities. A church should have specific procedures for getting the names of club visitors and church school parents into the evangelism file.

(4) *Church member contacts.* The friendship of church members with those outside the church is the greatest source of evangelistic outreach. Members must be urged not merely to submit names, but to give the first invitation themselves, and to report the result.

(5) *Less useful sources.* A neighborhood religious census is likely to be a waste of time because it is so easy to take but so hard to use. It should never be taken unless specific plans have already been made to follow up the contacts it makes. Members can check Welcome Wagon lists, new utility connections, and new public school enrollments. Such sources have some use, but they are far less useful than the contacts the church can make for itself.

The results of every approach and all relevant data are recorded in the file; cards should also include recommendations. No card is ever taken from the file for any purpose until it is permanently removed.

Progress

When a contact has been made, what then? Very few people, except those who have recently left another congregation, will be ready for church membership. If, by some charmed persuasion, newcomers could be brought at once into church membership, it would be a disaster for them and for the church. It has been argued that, in order to hold people, we should get them at once into the church where they will spend the rest of their lives learning what they need to know. The difficulty is that a stream does not rise above its source. If people start with a low estimate of what a Christian is, or what church membership requires, they are likely to remain there—if they remain at all. The required faith and vows are very simple, but also very searching. People should have some idea what the words mean when they say, "I accept Jesus Christ as my Lord and Savior" or, "I will strive to be a faithful member of the church."

An evangelism program must have long-range methods of pre-paring people for membership. It should try to get newcomers into the worship services, fellowship groups, classes, Koinonia groups, and social action task forces. It has to trust that in these will be found the strange, radical, world-shaking, world-forsaking, loving, and glorious reality of Christianity. The church can also provide books and pamphlets to provide the truth at various intellectual levels.

The approach may start with a phone call, which does no more than show a friendly interest—"Glad you were in church" or, "We heard you moved to this area." These calls find out whether there is any use in further contacts. Where there is, home calls are needed. These try to rouse interest in various sorts of church participation, and bring back recommendations for future steps. A letter can prepare for personal approaches, but by itself it does little good. The postman cannot do the churchman's work, but the church can do much to arouse interest. Having children in choirs brings nonmembers to church services. Ushers and greeters can help make a church attractive. Coffee and punch after services give a chance for meeting visitors and making them want to return. It helps if the building looks loved. Church organizations need an officer who receives in writing the names of those who might be interested, with a card for reporting what he does about the opportunity and the result. Here again, mailed invitations do little good except as preparation, and the telephone is inadequate. A concerned "Let me stop by for you" or, "I'll be looking for you at the door," is all that really works. Consider such questions as: Does the church have enough doors? Will one visit encourage a second look? Other entrance points are groups for young adults, for parent training, for community action, for prayer, or serious reading.

Commitment

When the newcomer has had an opportunity to learn about the Christian faith and life, and the meaning of church membership, and to feel the beauty and the splendor of it, then the question must be raised, "Is this for you?" Decisions are important. Psychology joins theology in holding that it makes a world of difference when people definitely make up their minds and say so. The Christian life cannot be a matter of "I suppose so" or, "Perhaps." The Bible again and again calls for commitment. Jesus said, "Every one who acknowledges me before men, I also will acknowledge before my Father who is in heaven" (Matt. 10:32). Paul said, "If you confess with your lips that Jesus is Lord, and believe in your heart that God raised him from the dead, you will be saved" (Rom. 10:9). Most of our days pass in uneventfulness, but there are some that tower up like mountain peaks. From them we get our bearings. It is the business of the church to bring such days. A life-governing decision needs to be expressed in words, and there needs to be some sign that puts it in the realm of tangible reality. Joining the church is such a sign.

The purpose of evangelism is not to bolster an institution. That temptation is always there, for we like to have a going concern. We do want to have the church, the body of Christ, present on as many scenes as possible. We want it to be a strong instrument for Him to use. But we also believe that God put His church on earth to give blessings that every human being needs. We want Christians in the church because we believe they need it. A religion whose key word is *love* requires fellowship.

There are countless circumstances in which a decision for the Christian faith may be expressed. The opportunity may present itself at a church service, a youth retreat, a communicants' class, in the pastor's study, or during a conversation in a home.

Evangelistic Calling

There are great advantages in having religious decisions made in homes. The most intimate questions are thus faced in the familiar surroundings, where a person can be most at ease. There will more likely be a sharing of thoughts with a caller whose coming shows he cares. A lay caller demonstrates the friendly interest of the members, whereas a minister is paid to make calls; his point of view is professional. "A jury discounts a paid witness," but a layman tells what his faith and his church mean to him from the layman's point of view. Also, only members have available the great number of hours evangelistic calls require. What is more, great benefits come to the callers. An evangelist must always be his own first convert.

Evangelistic visiting is not connected with any particular theology or era. It has always been important in the church, and always will be. It is equally useful for staid or "swinging" congregations, for pietists or activists. It is simply an ideal method of communicating whatever a church has to say. Depending on the motives of the people involved, it can be perfunctory or searching, manipulative or respectful, a smooth technique or an experience of how great it is when people get beyond superficialities and open up their hearts to each other.

If a church does not have many experienced callers, there are great advantages in arranging a program over several evenings in a row. If dates are made far enough ahead, it is as easy to engage callers for successive evenings as for scattered ones. New callers who are uncertain the first night can gain confidence on succeeding ones. The group can learn by discussing the calls of the night before. If there is supper and a meeting before the visiting, members can concentrate on training which progresses from one night to the next. A guest trainer can be engaged if the minister of the church wants a fresh voice.

Does this talk of "training" suggest learning how to overpower people? It is not that at all, but one must realize that callers can make mistakes if they have not considered them in advance. Contacts may expose sensitive areas, and there are possibilities of harm as well as good. The essential qualifications are faith and a love of people, but those will not save the caller who cannot think how to get a serious conversation started, or finds himself losing out to the television set. A voluble witness must learn to listen. Similar

situations keep presenting themselves, and callers can profit from
what others have learned across the years. We could make fun of
the idea of a manual for visitors, as though the teacher could run
his thumb down an index and find a pat answer for every question. But callers must give information and remove miscon-
ceptions. When someone says, "We don't think we should join
the church until we know how long we will be here" or, "I would
have become a church member long ago, but there is something in
the Apostles' Creed I don't believe," the visitor should not have to
improvise an answer as though such a response had never been
heard before.

The visitors know that these are not just social calls. They are
praying for decisions that will bring measureless blessings in all the
years ahead. Imposing a purpose may well intimidate them. They
may find it almost impossible to raise the significant questions
they have come to ask. Without help, many callers will never get
beyond saying, "We've got the best choir in town; don't you want
to join our church?"

If it is not possible to go calling on successive evenings, or if a
sufficient number of opportunities are not evident, a Sunday
afternoon and evening, or a weekday evening, may be best. New
callers may go out with those who have had experience. Even
experienced callers should have some preparation—no one ever
knows enough. The veterans need to renew their humility at the
greatness of the task. Simply to hand out assignments and send the
callers on their way is to arrange for failure. What they are trying
to achieve is something only God can do. They need a strong sense
of His presence and His help. Many a person who is asked to make
such calls replies, "That's not in my line; I'm just not cut out for
that sort of thing." They are quite right. But if they try it anyway,
they are likely to come back declaring it has been one of the
greatest experiences of their lives. In this they have had a clear
proof of the miraculous.

The committee will need one of the books or booklets on how
to arrange a calling program. This will explain how to enlist callers,
give suggestions for their instruction, and tell how assignments are
made.

Jesus "called . . . the twelve, and began to send them out two
by two" (Mark 6:7). The two-by-two plan is still best. More than
two may seem overpowering, but a lone visitor is not as impressive
as two, and he needs a helper. Some churches have a permanent

calling organization—"The St. Andrew's Fellowship," or "The Seventy." How often callers go out depends upon how often the list can be renewed. To have only a few calling programs a year works better for new member classes, but this may cause people who are ready to be seen to wait too long.

There are three quite different kinds of evangelical calls:

(1) Prospect calls show welcome, stir interest in particular church activities, and get information. Attractive personalities are important, but no special skills or knowledge are needed by the callers.

(2) Decision calls are made to those who may be ready to make decisions for Christian faith and church membership. These callers must be qualified, spiritually and intellectually.

(3) New member calls are made to welcome new members and to help them get a good start in the church.

Giving a Good Start

The most important part of evangelism comes after the decision has been made. No evangelistic decision was ever good enough. If the decision is supposed to mean birth into the new life in Christ, then one would have to say of all of them, "I don't believe in it." The decision can be of great importance. It can be the definite facing in a new direction, the finally saying Yes to Christ, and meaning it. But one of the church's most damaging mistakes is thinking that this moment of decision marks the entrance into the Christian fold. The most able preacher, the most dedicated caller, cannot, in the little time available, let people know just what it is they are deciding. The pressing need is to put content into the decision. Here are some of the next things to be done:

(1) *Minister's interview.* When callers come back with joyful news of positive response to the gospel, the minister needs to make an appointment to talk with prospective members. He wants to take them farther in their understanding of what their decisions mean; he must become their pastor and their friend.

(2) *New member class.* A class gives an incomparable opportunity for instructing, inspiring, and motivating at the time in life when these will mean the most. Prospective members are usually eager to know more about the Christian faith and life, about the

church and its history, about practices, attitudes, and duties, and about the life of the local church. Class sessions offer one of the best ways of validating a decision. They may change the minds of some who thought they were ready to join the church. Some churches require attendance at such classes. There need be no worry about making it too difficult to join the church—people want what is obviously important. It is strange when a boy has to do more to become a Tenderfoot Scout than an adult has to do to become a member of Christ's church. The new member class may serve as an inquirers' group for those who are still undecided. Written materials will be needed. In small churches the classes may have just one or two members—but this has advantages.

(3) *Youth communicant class*. Joining the church can be a momentous event for boys or girls. In preparing for it they will think more deeply and do more class work; they are also more easily reached emotionally than at any other time. A church which considers business-as-usual in the church school to be all the preparation needed for such a decision, throws away a priceless opportunity. In the past two decades the tendency has been for the number of such classes to increase to include people from ages six to forty, or even older. In this matter, other churches are coming to where the Lutherans have always been. Every boy or girl with whom the church has contact should at some time be asked to consider a profession of faith and joining the church. The age at which this should be presented, and the method of doing it, need to be determined. It can be done in a church school class, a youth group, a special service, or in a personal interview. Letters to the homes can ask for the parents' prayers and interest in this. We must be aware of the danger of making it appear that joining the church is an automatic next step for those who reach a certain age or complete the class. It must be a deeply felt personal decision, without group pressure. Near the end of the course of study there may be private conferences at which each pupil can talk with a minister or church officer about this great step, and whether or not to take it.

(4) *Literature*. Much that the new members need to know can be given them in books or pamphlets. This material should not be handed out all at once. With each piece there should be a personal word about why it is important.

(5) *Written Forms.* Those who join the church are asked to make the most profound statements the human mind can encompass, and the most binding vows. Therefore there must be a chance to think and pray about these in advance. That is why many churches have them printed on forms which can be pondered, and then signed. These same forms may have spaces for biographical information the church needs, such as a record of baptism and past church experiences, and a check list of services that can be offered to the church. A sheet may explain, step-by-step, how one joins the church. New members may be given membership certificates.

(6) *Joining.* Getting married and joining the church are the greatest occasions in any life. Both should be arranged so that they will be remembered ever after with gratitude and joy. When joining a church is perfunctory and hasty, to suit the convenience of officers or the minister, it is a travesty on the church and a dishonoring of the Holy Spirit. A great deal of thought should be given to ways of making this occasion solemn, impressive, and joyful. For example, a church officer may be assigned to sit with each new member and family. Those who are joining are presented, not just by name, but with some friendly personal details. There may be a welcoming talk with good advice. Representatives may describe various church activities and invite participation. Pledge cards may be presented and stewardship explained. Perhaps each new member could sign a historic covenant or roll book. There may be a tour of the church building. You may wish to take a group picture, and later post it so the new members can be identified. New members may be assigned to duties or task forces. They may make a statement of their faith and purposes. Then, as the church of Christ, you may wish to celebrate the Lord's Supper together. A social reception might be the last event.

At the public welcome before the congregation, there should be a sense of celebration. The new members may be called forward to answer questions about their faith and purposes, or to make statements in their own words. The congregation can pledge its love and care. The minister, in behalf of the congregation, may give new members the right hand of fellowship. Flowers or pins may be given the new members so they can be recognized and greeted afterwards. The minister may stand in the church aisle throughout this ceremony so the new and old members face each other. You may wish to have them stand at the door so other members can greet them on the way out. Certainly the lay officers could take much of the leadership in this ceremony.

No one church would do all these things. However, they are listed to suggest different ways small or large churches can make joining memorable.

(7) *Fellowship.* The natural laws of social life are against in-coming members. They think of the church as someone else's club into which they must not thrust themselves. And the love of Christians has a seamy side which makes the old members enjoy each other so much they have no time for newcomers. Unless church members work against these tendencies, new members may never make good friends in their new church. Likeable extroverts do well enough, but many people need a great deal of help.

Here, as with prospective members, group activities and classes have a big part to play. They receive the names of all new members and set their enrollment processes into operation, not counting on the mail or telephone, but making personal engage-ments for the first meetings. The committee's budget may provide guest tickets for dinner meetings.

(8) *Sponsors.* Everybody's business is nobody's, and the con-gregation's promise of "our Christian love and care," will die with the shaking of hands unless someone is designated to carry it out. Assigned sponsors should make calls or extend newcomers invita-tions to their homes. They can arrange to meet their new members at the church and introduce them to others. However, this plan works well only when someone sponsors the sponsors. If there are neighborhood parish divisions, the parish leaders may be the sponsors.

(9) *Pledges.* Getting the new members' pledges is important, not because the church is eager for their money, but because it is eager for their hearts, and Jesus' saying is still true, "Where your treasure is, there will your heart be also" (Matt. 6:21). Those who have a weak financial relationship with a church are likely to be hard to hold and hard to please. New members need guidance. If they are expected to guess how much the pledge should be, the guess may be a poor one. Stewardship methods and motives can be explained in the new member class, at the time of joining, by house calls, and in writing. The first pledge sets the level for the future, and it should not be delayed.

(10) *Service.* Members never really feel that "their church" is "my church" until some of their lives are built into it through giving their time and effort. New members are reluctant to check a list for how to offer their services, unless they are prompted. Churches must avoid the danger that the record for proffered services will be left in a file, with the new members feeling rejected because they were not asked for what they offered to do. Sometimes certain regular services are reserved for new members—such as leading the responsive reading, delivering flowers to the ill, helping in the financial canvass.

(11) *Status Check.* The list of all who have joined during the past two or three years should be checked regularly to locate any who are getting a weak start. This situation may be remedied if it is caught soon enough, but before long it becomes incurable.

The saddest duty in any church is the removal, from the roll, of the names of those who can no longer be considered active members. When this is done the mood is likely to be critical— "They were poor members" or, "They did not keep their promises." If those under criticism were on hand to answer, as they usually are not, they might reply, "The church did not keep its promises to us. Where was all that friendship and help we heard about? We were left to sink or swim, so we sank." The ultimate success or failure of evangelism depends most on what is done *after* people join the church.

For the Church

Karl Barth said that when a church quits evangelizing "it begins to smell of the 'sacred,' to play the priest and mumble. Anyone with a keen nose will smell it and find it dreadful." A congregation turned in upon itself tends to become stiff and cold and formal. Reaching out to others is the surest source of new life in a church. It forces a church to think of what its essential purposes are, and of how well it is achieving them. "For their sake I consecrate myself" (John 17:19). The power of the Holy Spirit is not given to those who, with folded hands, are looking up to heaven, waiting for a visitation. It is given to those whose hands have taken up a work for God that is impossible without His help. The effort to make the Christian faith plain for others is what best makes it clear for the members of a church. "Evangelize or fossilize" is still the law.

It is beneficial if these answers to the question, "What can we do about evangelism?" have made it seem a large task. The unchanging rule is, *Shortcuts in evangelism never work.* Only a congregation whose gratitude, love for God, and love for man impel it to carry through the whole long process, will ever have, or deserve to have, the great reward. That reward is to see people and homes radiant with the wonder and the beauty of the love of Jesus Christ.

Let's Take to the Air 7

THE RADIO OPPORTUNITY IN EVANGELISM

Joel Nederhood

Churches on the North American continent have a very efficient tool for reaching their neighbors and the entire world with the gospel. That tool is radio, and up until this century, God's people never had anything like it. Theoretically, television is available as well, but there is evidence it is encumbered with enough built-in problems to insure that its use by the church will be the exception, at least for the present.[1] But radio offers the church a particularly versatile medium that is unrivaled in terms of economy—the experience of some broadcasters indicates that radio may well achieve one personal exposure for every penny spent.

There is a certain natural usefulness about radio when it comes to gospel proclamation. It is virtually distortion free, for the word, spoken or sung, comes to the listener just as it was first delivered. And radio adapts itself automatically to the way the gospel was first communicated when it started to spread out from Jerusalem nearly two millenia ago. There was a swift, assault-like quality about much of the church's early mission, an in-and-out movement by the apostles and their aides that bore rich fruit in spite of the relatively limited personal contact. Radio can be an audacious instrument for gospel proclamation that duplicates something of

[1] John Ferguson's article, "A Christian in the Open University," *WAAC Journal*, March, 1970, p. 20, presents a useful comparison of the relative

73

the same movement, today; in doing so, it can penetrate inaccessible places very efficiently.

Perhaps radio's capability of duplicating something of the apostolic dynamic needs to be underscored. For thoughtful Christians are rightfully demanding something more than Christian words. Today, all of us know that a Christianity that does not develop a unique life-style will be unsatisfactory in the long run. This fairly recent rediscovery of the life-changing power of the Christian message might dilute the church's interest in using radio. Radio, after all, seems capable only of speaking the gospel and does not seem able to demonstrate Christian love.

Our current interest in Christianity as a Spirit-dominated way of life should not make us forget that the early Christian communities were created by the Spirit of God who used the "announcement" of the gospel message as the primary tool. There is a power that resides in the message of God's great work in Jesus, a power that continues to operate no matter how deformed the Christian community may be at any given moment. And we know now that all our talk of communication through personal contact and community impact is still significantly neutralized by certain sociological realities that apparently can hardly be overcome. So the message as such must be presented ceaselessly. Paul did that. As he said to the Galatians, he set Christ crucified before their eyes (Gal. 3:1). And he seized upon the figure of a "sounding board" to describe the way the apostolic witness radiated out from local

values of television and radio when used to communicate educational materials. It is significant that in connection with the open university experiment in Britain, radio has proven to be most versatile and generally most usable.

The whole role of television use in gospel proclamation is a subject in itself. Up to this time, however, the most successful uses of this medium have been in terms of spectaculars or specials, programs which local churches, because of the nature of the case, cannot possibly produce. The general production demands and cost factors of television are such that, in most cases, local congregations should concentrate their efforts in other directions.

On the theoretical level, there are interesting questions that arise in connection with television as a communication medium. In my judgment, I feel that more and more evidence will gradually be collected to substantiate the thesis that television is basically not a communication medium since it must of necessity distort what it is communicating. Television is an entertainment medium, indeed, and possibly also an art form. But whether it is as much a communication medium as we generally assume it to be is open to question. A recent article appearing in *Life* tends to substantiate these general impressions ("Television" Daniel J. Boorstin, *Life*, Sept 10, 1971, pp. 36-39).

congregations (I Thess. 1:8, Phillips). When we talk about sounding boards we are getting very near what happens when a church uses radio to tell the world about Jesus.

Radio's appropriateness for evangelism is also clarified when we remember that a church that uses it is not just talking. By using a tool like radio, a church demonstrates its Christianity, too. It takes effort, talent, and possibly a good deal of money to use radio well, and a church that does this is demonstrating its seriousness and its sincere interest in sharing the gospel with others. The very use of radio is an act, a deed that demonstrates the vitality of a church's conviction and the unselfishness of its love.

Though radio offers the church an exceptionally useful tool for gospel proclamation, obviously not every local congregation will be able to use it to the same extent. There are, I suppose, two general attitudes a church might possibly develop with respect to its use of radio. The first attitude would amount to virtual disinterest, caused by limited personnel and budget along with many other responsibilities. Perhaps this attitude will prevail in most churches. The practical realities of some churchs' situations will simply force them to put radio work rather low on their scale of priorities. This attitude with respect to radio should not be criticized, for it is usually dictated by circumstances beyond the control of the local congregation.

On the other hand, there are also churches that should order their priorities so that their obligation to reach their community by means of radio is near the top of their concerns. This would be natural in larger congregations where the minister, or one of the ministers, has special gifts for radio communication. Possibly such a church would also have members who could help in program production. Such churches would hopefully develop a more serious interest in the possibilities radio offers. The material that follows is designed to help such churches approach the challenge of radio usefully.

However a church uses radio, it must remember that the term *radio* does not refer primarily to receivers and transmitters, the hardware we visualize when the word *radio* is used. Radio is an industry, in fact it is a sub-industry within the larger industry of broadcasting. A church will use radio intelligently only if it knows where the industry is at any given moment. An article that recently appeared in *Broadcasting,* titled "On the leading edge of broadcasting," is one of the most extensive single descriptions of the industry.[2] (The church that broadcasts regularly should subscribe to a publication like *Broadcasting.*)

When we look at the industry at this time, it is clear that for the foreseeable future, radio is going to be very big and exciting. Right now there are more than seven thousand stations in the United States that broadcast to more receivers than there are people. Radio is massive, carefully formulated, and highly segmented. Its sheer size is expressed in the more than fifty signals that come into the major markets during the daytime and in the jungle of sounds that boom around the country at night when the sky waves bring WWL—"way down yonder in New Orleans"—into the cab of the trucker heading out of Chicago to St. Louis at midnight.

Within the nearly overwhelming number of stations, each one has its own individuality. The "in" word now is *demographics,* the description of a station's target audience, and demographics now dictates what is going on in radio at the moment. In terms of demographic theory, each station carves out its share of the market and guards it jealously. It can tell you whether it is shooting for the fourteen- to nineteen-year-olds, the nineteen- to twenty-nine-year-olds, or the twenty-four- to thirty-nine-year-olds, and it is able to juggle the ratings around to prove that it is getting such and such percent of that market. Though there is most likely a good deal of self-deception in all the figures, there is enough substance to them to make them worth considering when a church considers which station it will use (assuming it has a choice).

Once a church has selected a station with suitable demographics, it can decide which route it will take so far as programming is concerned. There are several. Let's try to distinguish between them.

Broadcast of Worship Services. This is the simplest form of church broadcasting, and it can be useful when the demographics of a station coincide with the demographics of a church's membership. If the station used is a Christian station, for example, many of its listeners will expect to be able to hear several full worship services on Sunday. Though this kind of programming takes the least production effort, the minister does well to keep his material within the time limits and he should not include material in his sermons that violate broadcasting codes.

While the programming demands of this kind of presentation

---

2 *Broadcasting,* "Special Report—Radio '71," pp. 41-80.

are minimal, broadcasts of a worship service can be greatly en-
hanced by the addition of some small production techniques. The
minister may want to make certain comments directly to the radio
audience, and he could go out of his way to give a brief description of something happening in the service which the radio audience cannot see. A useful technique is to have an announcer work
right with the service, introducing it and signing off. He could also
speak during the offering and tell the listening audience something
about the church and the services it offers the community. Such
production techniques will sustain listener interest during periods
when what goes on within the sanctuary does not lend itself to an
interesting use of the broadcasting medium.

Modification of Worship Services. If it is possible for a church
to edit tapes of the services, it can produce a program package that
uses the components of the regular worship service, but which
presents a somewhat different sound. If the minister's message can
be brought into a fifteen-minute or twenty-minute length (using
tape editing if necessary), this message, along with high quality
musical elements of the liturgy, or even with the use of standard
available music, can present a tighter, faster moving broadcast
package than a regular worship service could provide.

A church that would be willing to spend the effort to produce
this kind of program could expect great interest on the part of the
stations. If there are resources available for doing this kind of
work, the results will be well worth the effort.

Feature Programs. Stations are always looking for feature programs—materials from two to five to fifteen minutes in length that
they can slip into a broadcast day to provide a change of pace and
heighten interest. If a church would look over its resources carefully, it might well find individuals who could produce features on
behalf of the church. For example, if a church has a counseling
ministry, the minister who does the counseling might prepare a
five-minute program that would highlight marital problems and
present a Christian perspective on such problems. Or a group of
young people might be able to produce a program that tells about
some of the new Christian youth music that is becoming more
plentiful lately. A commentary on the news, from a Christian
point of view, could also be useful.

If a church is any size at all, there are most likely possibilities
along the line of feature programs. However, they must be produced carefully and should have authority and professional quali-

ty. Whatever is done will go far in establishing the church's presence within the community and will, thus, increase its effectiveness as it brings the gospel.

Specials. If a church brings in a special lecturer or musical group, it can arrange to have this appearance broadcast. Special Easter and Christmas programs, if produced by professional standards, can be welcome additions to a station's programming schedule. This sharing of special programs declares the church's willingness to share all of its resources with the community, and thus contributes to its ministry.

Spot Announcements. Stations are especially interested in well-produced thirty-second and one-minute spot announcements that hit some special problem hard or tell something important quickly and well. A business man who had experienced the value of radio spots in advertising his products, encouraged his minister to produce spots for young people in a major Midwest market. These made a great impact upon the young people in that area and were later syndicated; WOR, a pace-setter station in the industry, picked them up for broadcast in the New York City market.[3] This is an example of what can be done, if a church is willing to make the effort.

Personalized Syndicated Materials. There are also many materials produced on the national level that can be tailor-made for use by a local congregation. For example, Chicago-based Racom Productions distributes a number of program materials that carry no identification and that can be played locally with the tag line of the local church. These consist of minute spot announcements, thirty-second television spots, and four and one-half- and fifteen-minute radio programs.[4] TRAFCO, the broadcasting arm of the United Methodist Church, located in Nashville, also has a wide variety of broadcasting materials. The American Bible Society has such materials as well.

If a denomination has a nationally produced radio program, it can often be adapted by the local congregation so that it has a distinctively local sound. The local minister might close off the broadcast with information about his church.

[3] This radio venture was carried on by the Rev. Wilbert Van Dyke, of the Plymouth Heights Christian Reformed Church, Grand Rapids, Michigan.

[4] RACOM PRODUCTIONS, 10858 S. Michigan Avenue, Chicago, Illinois, 60628.

This imaginative use of nationally produced materials will relieve the local church of many of the production headaches that are part of broadcasting and at the same time will give it a strong image in the community. Localizing national materials this way may take a little negotiation and ingenuity, but few broadcast efforts will pay off with richer dividends.

These possibilities all suggest directions a congregation can take if it decides to use radio to increase its ministry. The direction a church takes will depend upon the community it is in, the stations available, and, above all, the resources of the congregation itself. There must be resources in a church to do a creditable job of broadcasting, otherwise the job is better left undone. We have enough poorly conceived and produced religious broadcasting. We need no more. But skillfully produced material that presents the gospel of Christ effectively can make a powerful impact.

One thing is certain: local churches should be encouraged to use broadcasting if at all possible. For they possess certain advantages that national programs do not have. They have the advantage of personal contact with station management, and they can cultivate good relationships with the station over a period of time. In addition, stations are often interested in programming that originates locally. If nothing else, the use of such programs can be used to convince the Federal Communications Commission that a station takes its community responsibilities seriously.

Local churches are in an advantageous position price-wise when it comes to market penetration. At least they will always be entitled to local rates, which are generally 10 to 15 percent less than national scale. In addition, they are in line for receiving some of the free public service time most stations make available to local groups. This means that a local church can negotiate with great advantage as it approaches local stations with its plans. The advantages a local church has in broadcasting should be exploited to the full.

The incentive for such use of broadcasting must come from two sources. First of all, there must be an excitement within the local congregation about the use of radio. And if the older people don't have this, the younger people most likely will, for they use radio and know what it can do. There can be no real question about radio being the "leading edge" of broadcasting, as the article in *Broadcasting* calls it and proves to be true. Smart advertisers know the advantages of radio; more of their dollars are flowing radio's way, making over a third of the stations fat with profits.

The second source of incentive, and the most important, must be the irresistible compulsion the church should feel to use every means to bring the gospel to its community. Fortunately, few churches now are satisfied with addressing themselves solely to needs that arise out of their own lives exclusively. Those who know the saving power of God revealed in Jesus Christ, must look out and reach out. They are, like Paul, debtors to all. In an age of towering secularism and the dehumanization of mankind, the gospel alone has a message that can reverse the trends that are leading us all to destruction.

The church that feels the apostolic compulsion and that has been blessed with rich gifts will use radio with joy and will be amazed often because of the results God will give.

Togetherness
Has Advantages
8

THE EVANGELISM OF MASS CRUSADERS

John Wesley White

A mass evangelistic crusade is the uniting of the churches of an area for the purpose of presenting Christ to the people of their community through the media of a large-scale preaching mission. They necessarily must engage an evangelistic team, set dates, arrange for a commodious meeting place, and get set for a monumental amount of old-fashioned faith and elbow grease. The watchword of all this is *togetherness*.

At a time when psychiatrist Jean Rosenbaum calculates that "loneliness" is America's greatest killer of those who die between the ages of two and thirty-seven and that 94 percent of the people suffer from chronic alienation, is it any wonder that togetherness is the quest of our age? The vibrations of Bobby Sherman's song, "Getting Together," resound among the young around the world. "Putting it all together" is the current cliché used by championship coaches before the network cameras to explain a team's sudden ascent from mediocrity to excellence.

Togetherness and evangelism were uppermost in St. Paul's scale of priorities. "That there be no divisions among you; but that ye be perfectly joined *together* in the same mind," as "labourers *together* with God" (I Cor. 1:10; 3:9*), was the ideal the apostle Paul had for the evangelism of that ancient metropolis of Corinth. A divided church is like a wounded soldier on the battlefield. A

*References are to the King James Version.

united church which ignores evangelism is like a healthy soldier
without a gun. John A. Mackay, a founder of the World Council of
Churches, now laments that "unity is not for mission. Unity is for
unity." Hence, W. A. Visser t'Hooft, Secretary-General during
most of its existence, decries that the Council is presently in a
state where "confusion reigns supreme—politically, theologically,
socially."

Conversely, mission without the unity of the Spirit is unyielding. So togetherness is essential if a mass evangelistic crusade is to
have a fruitful impact upon a community. Carl F. H. Henry saw
this in a *Christianity Today* editorial in 1967 when he wrote the
article, "Somehow Let's Get Together" which triggered into existence the "Key Bridge Evangelism, '73" crusades. As they sped
toward realization, their executive director, Theodore Raedke,
reflected the necessity "for Christians to mount a new initiative in
evangelism—*together.*"

Togetherness—this, to me, is the distinguishing feature of the
mass evangelistic crusade in the world today. It occurs when the
members of the body of Christ in a given area **premeditate together.** I like to think of the disciples on the road to Emmaus. As
they walked along a country road they were as dejected and
disillusioned as are many in the church today. When "they com-
muned *together* and reasoned, Jesus drew near and went with
them" (Luke 24:15). That was one of the initiating encounters in
fellowship which led to the mass evangelism of Pentecost. It was
where "brethren dwell *together* in unity" that, in ancient times as
today, "the Lord commanded the blessing" (Ps. 133:1, 3). "This is
the blessing," wrote Moses, when the tribes of Israel were
gathered together (Deut. 33:1). When was the last time in your
community or mine that the people of God "took sweet counsel
together" (Ps. 55:14), that "the whole church" in your area came
"*together* into one place" (I Cor. 14:23), for purposes of sharing?
We mingle at so many different intersections today: socially,
academically, recreationally, politically, and in connection with
our jobs. Why not a getting together of true believers in Christ? In
fact, St. Paul said, "Be ye not unequally yoked *together* with
unbelievers: for what fellowship hath righteousness with unrigh-
teousness? and what communion hath light with darkness?" (II
Cor. 6:14). "Can two walk *together* except they be agreed?" asked
Amos (3:3). It is a sin not to "love the brotherhood" (I Peter
2:17). How tragically often it happens that genuine disciples of

Jesus deny themselves the blessing of Christian communion with each other, simply because they have never sought each other out as spiritual brothers. I have met with the General Committees of our Billy Graham Associate Evangelistic Crusades around the world, often in small places, as well as with those of Mr. Graham's major crusades, and invariably I have observed that the germination of the crusade began when believers, perhaps of diverse doctrinal persuasion, but of like precious faith, got together initially for fellowship.

I was staying in Niagara Falls, New York, for a few days, and, walking down the sidewalk rather absentmindedly, I stumbled into a pile of bricks. I stepped back and saw a sign I had missed. It read: "Sidewalk Closed; Take Street." And I thought: what an impediment to the way which leads to life the brickbats of a crumbling quarreling church must be, in any community! "If you throw mud," said Adlai Stevenson, "you lose ground." How much more this is true in the church of Jesus Christ.

We will go nowhere together in premeditation, however, until we **pray together.** Action in the Acts of the Apostles swung on the watchword that the frontiersmen of Christianity "were gathered praying" (Acts 12:12). Still reeling in the stunning realization that Jesus was alive, the apostles were not hesitant to invoke His guidance: "When they therefore were come *together,* they asked of him . . . " (Acts 1:6). They had heard His assurance that "where two or three are gathered *together* in my name, there am I in the midst of them" (Matt. 18:20). It was a promise for all time. In the days of Jehoshaphat when a people were in deep trouble, "Judah gathered . . . *together* to ask help of the Lord" (II Chron. 20:4); in Isaiah's day, the concerned people resolved, "Let us plead *together*" (Isa. 43:26); in Ezra's, it was when "the priests and the Levites were purified *together*" (Ezra 6:20) and settled on the primacy of prayer that Israel's heritage was restored and her foes vanquished. "Helping *together* by prayer for us" (II Cor. 1:11), was the undertaking for which Paul commended the Corinthians. A mass evangelistic crusade which is not born and borne in prayer, is as unyielding as a crop which is planted, only to die because of all sunshine and no rain. All sunshine and no rain creates a desert. Pour out the tears of concerned intercession on any community and it will ripen for a spiritual harvest. Mr. Graham's Tokyo Crusade in 1967 involved five thousand home prayer meetings; his London crusades of the 1966 and '67 era rolled on the wheels of ten thousand prayer meetings in the Greater London area alone. Supplementing these were such prayer meetings around the world as four hundred believers in an African leprosarium, rising at 4:00 A.M. to pray together for the lost millions of London. I witnessed a most fruitful harvest in Gibson City, Illinois, which, I suspect, owed more to the fact that at regular intervals two farmers got off their tractors at specified fenceposts and knelt in the loamy soil for prayer than to any of the huge billboards which heralded the news of the crusade along the main highways. Such prayers fill the clouds with showers of blessing. Sow in tears; reap in joy.

Just as love must precede a proposal for marriage, so if there is to be a divinely-ordained area-wide evangelistic crusade, prayer must precede the proposal for such an undertaking. Prayer never ends with the praying. It inspires action. Often when believers bound together by geographical proximity are also bound together in prayer, they will **propose together**. The Lord commissioned Moses at the burning bush: "Go gather the elders of Israel *together*" (Exod. 3:16), and so was initiated the campaign for Israel's mass exodus from Egypt. Before the great ingathering of three thousand on the day of Pentecost, "there were *together* Simon Peter," and "other of his disciples," with Peter proposing, "I go a fishing" (John 21:2, 3). Fishing he went, but instead of a physical catch, his Lord intervened and gave him a spiritual net which gathered in a multitude. The coming of Jesus was to "gather *together* in one the children of God that were scattered" (John 11:52). This had been the divine model from antiquity. Jeremiah (50:4) proclaimed, "Israel and Judah shall come *together*"—they had split into factions. As believers, God has "raised us up *together*, and made us sit *together* in heavenly places in Christ Jesus" (Eph. 2:6). If we "sit together in heavenly places in Christ Jesus," why is it that we cannot stand together on earth with Christ Jesus, in a united presentation of the gospel to a given community? In my experience, togetherness has been responsible, in city after city, in metropolitan area after metropolitan area, in county after county, for the initiation of an invitation to an evangelist, which in turn has resulted in a fruitful crusade.

Proposing together, by a body of Christians, to hold a united evangelistic crusade for Christ will find practical reality when they **project together**. History is littered with dreamers who never did, and doers who never dreamed. When the vision is decoded and translated into reality, when the idea which has been divinely conceived is enacted through human obedience, a worthwhile united crusade is conducted. There must be a plan, a divine blueprint, which the early apostles called *the will of God,* if brethren in Christ in a specified area are to sponsor an evangelistic crusade. It is then and then only that they can plan the work and work the plan fruitfully. So a Christian—clergyman or layman, prominent or inconspicuous—starts the wheels rolling, looking for the Lord to "put them *together* as the sheep" (Mic. 2:12), while at the same time taking the initiative: "gather my saints *together* unto me" (Ps. 50:5). Jesus wept over an ancient metropolis: "O Jerusalem, Jerusalem, thou that killest the prophets, and stonest them which are sent unto thee, how often would I have gathered thy children *together,* even as a hen gathereth her chickens under her wings, and ye would not!" (Matt. 23:37). I wonder how many cities there are which have never, in this generation, had anyone weep over them with the compassion of Jesus. Again and again, the story of a successful crusade goes back to how the foundations for a great crusade were laid: a group had prayed. They had seen an evangelist, perhaps on television, or even gone as a delegation to one of the great crusades. They felt the impact of the spiritual happening. They initiated an invitation to an evangelist. Ahead of time they had a vision of what could take place in their area. They invited all those of mutual vision and concern to consider . . . *together.* In the hearts of some they found ashes; in others, sparks; and in still others, leaping flames like their own. And so the evangelist—or his organizer—met with them. A general committee was formed and an overall plan adopted. But it takes a miracle for the confusion of many minds to be fused into the mind of Christ.

Those who have proposed an area crusade must **prepare together**: God has always implemented His will through men who are ready to "prepare the way of the Lord." Jesus used the technique of sending disciples ahead to prepare certain places for His coming. The general committee of the crusade will have to demonstrate real consecration if they are regularly to "take counsel *together*" (Isa. 45:21). They will have to lay claim to their oneness in Christ. They will have to look up for guidance, "from whom the whole body fitly joined *together* and compacted by that which every joint supplieth . . . maketh increase of the body . . . " (Eph. 4:16). And someone will emerge as the ostensible leader, as in Ezra's day: "Then stood Jeshua with . . . his brethren . . . *together,* to set forward the workmen in the house of

God . . . " (Ezra 3:9). A general committee needs a chairman, and, meeting with him regularly throughout the entire preparation, operation, and preservation phases of the crusade, an executive committee. This cabinet body will consist of chairmen of the working committees which are responsible for the prayer, publicity, Operation Andrew, counseling, ushers, music, arrangements, finance, youth, public relations, and follow-up phases of the crusade. The size and composition of this executive committee of working chairmen differs, of course, from area to area. But the function is essentially the same in all crusades.

So an integral part of crusade preparation is to **program together**. The Lord of the harvest has a program for each crusade. Take the area of music. If, in God's tuning of creation, "the morning stars sang *together*" (Job 38:7), He can surely blend a heterogeneous collection of church singers into a crusade choir. "Sing *together*," exhorted Isaiah; "with the voice *together* they shall sing" (52:8, 9). In the wilderness Israel ran out of water. So Jehovah bade Moses "gather thou the assembly *together*" (Num. 20:8). When their need was met, we read, "then Israel sang the song: spring up, O well, sing ye." Virtually all of the Billy Graham musicians are frequently asked, "Do you take that choir with you from city to city?" Perhaps they have only met a few times, but for mutual believers in Christ there is an immediate harmony which God the Holy Spirit generates.

Early in preparation and until the adopted budget has been met, an area-wide crusade will need to **consider the cost together**. There is, of course, the price of dedicated involvement, and this is by far the highest cost in any crusade. The whole of the Christian life is one in which, as St. Paul taught, "we suffer with him, that we may also be glorified *together*" (Rom. 8:17); and again: " . . . if we have been planted *together* in the likeness of his death, we shall be also in the likeness of his resurrection" (Rom. 6:5). This is to effect the process of growing together in Christ, "in whom all the building fitly framed *together* groweth unto an holy temple in the Lord: in whom ye also are builded *together* for an habitation of God through the Spirit" (Eph. 2:21, 22). I have never yet heard of an executive committee which experienced no thorny situations. Discipleship has always demanded the bearing of the cross. Coming up roses involves occasional tensions and wholesome differences of opinion in order to arrive at syntheses of judgments. Job, thousands of years ago, admonished, "We should come *together* in judgment" (Job 9:32). Out of such vigorous mixes will come the batter from which crusades are baked.

But then, of course, there is the financial price. And for this, there is the glorious promise of Jesus which, taken at its face value, always works: "Give, and it shall be given unto you; good measure pressed down, and shaken together and running over, shall men give into your bosom!" (Luke 6:38). A budget must be carefully planned, raised, spent, and accounted for by the local executive committee. This is their task.

Can a community afford a united evangelistic crusade? The more relevant question is: when the will of Christ is revealed that it should have one, can it afford not to have one? The American gross national product is a trillion dollars. Eleven times as much is spent on crime as on all forms of religion. Yet, in Greenville, South Carolina, six months after Mr. Graham's crusade there, it was reported that crime was down 50 percent—this in addition to the thousands of decisions for Christ. At this moment in American history, the average cost to the state of one youth going astray is $50,000. The salvation of one life will thus pay for two average Billy Graham Associate Crusades; the salvation of twenty young people on this basis would pay for a Billy Graham Television Crusade reaching an aggregate of a hundred million people. On the average, it costs about ninety cents for each person who attends a Billy Graham major or associate crusade. The cost to the average church for each person who enters the building is about $2.50. These are financial facts that need to be considered. God's work is always costly. But left undone, man soon loses his way, his world, and his hopes for the heaven Jesus went to prepare.

In today's world a crusade committee must **promote together.** Paul bade the Philippians to "stand fast in one spirit, with one mind striving *together* for the faith of the gospel" (1:27); and to the Colossians he described how the body, being "knit *together,* increaseth with the increase of God" (2:19). When a crusade committee knows that they have been called of God to undertake a crusade, they have a sure promise: "We know that all things work *together* for good to them that love God, to them who are the called according to his purpose" (Rom. 8:28). So the job of publicity is not merely another job; it is a call from heaven. With this kind of mandate, what person can fail to be inspired to produce, circulate, or display bumper or lapel stickers, window signs, crusade banners, billboard advertisements, and newspaper, radio, and television announcements? He can do this when he realizes that the cause is for Jesus Christ who gave His all and held back nothing. While effective advertising of a crusade does not, on its own, assemble a crowd of people, it does condition the people of an area to respond to the more direct approaches of crusade proponents and to attend.

Crusade participants must **propagate together**: One means of transmitting the gospel is by personal visitation from house to house. In the Billy Graham Crusade in Tokyo, in 1967, every home in that metropolis of eleven million was visited prior to the crusade. Just how colossal an undertaking this was and what it accomplished can be seen in the fact that while Tokyo had only a total of fifteen thousand Christians, the nightly attendance at the crusade averaged fifteen thousand. Another means of propagation is by every conceivable improvisation of Operation Andrew. It can be as effective today as it was in Biblical times. To signal the resurrection, "Peter . . . and that other disciple . . . ran both *together*" (John 20:3, 4). Peter himself had initially been won to Jesus when his brother Andrew had gone to fetch him. Consider also the young. In our Billy Graham crusades 83 percent of all inquirers are under the age of twenty-one. Youth have always banded together and gone out to make their influence felt. From the time "young men . . . rose up and went *together*" (Gen. 22:19) right through the centuries to the current Jesus revolution, youth have worked together with God in witness. So it is incumbent on those who are responsible for visitation to see that the various age levels of concerned people "are gathered *together* . . . to serve the Lord" (Ps. 102:22)—be they individuals, pairs, or groups of eager youth. They go out on behalf of Christ to wherever people live, work, study, or play, to interest them in using the crusade as a vehicle for their evangelism. The recruitment of bodies of people, including large percentages of unbelievers, to attend the crusade in delegations or blocks is the undertaking of the Operation Andrew committee. Of those who become enquirers in Billy Graham associate crusades, 55 percent are actually brought by concerned Christians, 40 percent were influenced to attend by Christians, and only 5 percent attended on the basis of having seen the crusade advertised. So Operation Andrew is incalculably important in any crusade.

Just before the opening night, when the counselors are trained, the choir formed, and the ushers mobilized, the churches should have a Crusade Sunday in which all pastors so inclined **preach together** on the objectives, meaning, and relevance of the crusade. A sort of "His troops come *together*" (Job 19:12) Sunday on which word on the crusade is shared. It is important—extremely important—that there be an understanding that the Lord has apointed many—not one only—to share the gospel with the needy in a crusade community. Because "thou hast also appointed prophets to preach," exulted Nehemiah, we "take counsel *together*" (6:7). An interdenominational crusade has meaning in a community only as it is related to the churches of that community. However thoroughly the work of preparation has been done, most of the people in participating churches who come to the Sunday services immediately preceding the crusade are still unaware of what a crusade is all about. The wise pastor will spell out that meaning in simple and vigorous language. This also helps the pastor himself to clarify his objectives concerning involvement in the crusade. A Sunday spent in this manner can enormously enhance the fruitfulness which will accrue to that church as an outcome of the crusade.

Opening night, and the three hundred, three thousand, or thirty thousand gather. It is in the time for the nightly gospel **proclamation together**. It may seem as it did to John Mark (1:33) when Jesus began His public ministry, that "all the city was gathered together at the door." Times do not change, when it comes to the human element, nearly as much as we sometimes think. You might imagine you are reading the *Oakland Tribune* regarding the Billy Graham Crusade there in July, 1971, when you open your Bible to Nehemiah 7:66 (Ezra 2:64 has precisely the same statement) and read, "The whole congregation *together* was forty and two thousand, three hundred and threescore." There are other salients of history that never change: "both low and high, rich and poor," observed the ancient psalmist, "[gather] *together*" (49:2); and certainly Jeremiah had an observation that might have caught the eye of an *Oakland Tribune* reporter with comparable admiration: They "rejoice, . . . both young men and old *together*" (31:13). The generation gap closes in a crusade. God is the best host in His universe, and when He invites men to be His guests to share the hospitality of His Word of salvation, there is no experience like it! There is an explanation of what it is that draws thousands to Christ in a crusade; it is Emmanuel—God with us. And so the inquirers respond, and the counselors deal with them. It is signifi-

cant that the percentage of those who respond to the invitation in
Billy Graham crusades is increasing as the decades pass. During the
1940s about 2 percent responded; during the '50s, it was about 3
percent; during the '60s, 4 percent; and now in the '70s, it is
leveling at about 5 percent (nearly 7 percent in Oakland).

Who are these enquirers? A study of those who respond in Billy
Graham crusades indicates that of every thousand who go forward,
on average there are six hundred students in school or university,
two hundred housewives, one hundred laborers, fifty children,
twenty career women, ten businessmen, ten men in other profes-
sions, two doctors, two high school teachers, two university pro-
fessors, a lawyer, a policeman, and a few who defy categorization.

Then, it is the privilege and obligation of the church to **preserve
together**. I remember a critic asking Dr. J. Brown Hendry, chairman of a united crusade in Glasgow years ago, "Can these babes
walk?" and he, a physician, replied that although he had delivered
hundreds of babies, he had never yet seen a newborn baby walk,
not until another eight or ten months had elapsed. The immediate
postnatal development of new converts is absolutely crucial. They
watch other believers for an example, and they need fellowship in
the worship and life of service in a church, right from the outset.
"Brethren, be followers *together* of me," St. Paul exhorted young
Philippian believers (3:17). "Draw near *together* ye that are es-
caped," exhorted Isaiah (45:20). New converts are urged not to
forsake "the assembling of [themselves] *together*" (Heb. 10:25).
The newborn spiritually must be informed that they have been
"quickened *together* with him" (Col. 2:13), and this means a regular
adherence to Christ's ordinances for grace and growth. Recipro-
cally, the church will want to share enthusiastically with these
eager rookies the three essential communications of the believer:
with Christ in prayer, Him with them through systematic study of
the Scriptures, and they with others. They must understand that
the more they share Christ, the more they will be aware they have
Christ to share. Then they will grow in grace and into the life of
the church.

From an area-wide crusade, each church which has enthusiastically cooperated ought, with the others, to **profit together**.
Churches should resolve with the ancient Ezra, "we ourselves
together will build" (4:3); and build they will. Over and over again
in I Corinthians 11:18 we read, "Come *together* in the church."
Paul adds the recommendation, "Come not *together* unto condem-

nation" (I Cor. 11:34), but for edification. A new convert is often alienated because some believer expects mature Christian conduct from him, when he has only newly begun with Christ. Comprehensive and compassionate follow-up with converts by the churches to which they have been referred will bring immense dividends. A Presbyterian pastor in Australia who participated in Mr. Graham's Sydney Crusade in 1959 made a careful survey of referrals. Of 646 referrals, 150 were already church members, while 404 sought and obtained membership. In 1968, I was told that of the 404 who became church members 52 percent were regular worshipers, 24 percent were "fairly regular," and 24 percent could not be accounted for.

In mid-1971, a Jesuit priest, Charles Dullea, superior of The Biblical Institute in Rome published his *W. F. "Billy" Graham's Decisions for Christ.* Conceding that his study which had taken three years was incomplete, Dr. Dullea in an interview stressed that the results of Mr. Graham's crusades are to be seen wherever one turns. Perhaps a study of the grandchildren and great-grandchildren of the crusades would reveal even greater results than a study of the actual converts.

I recently held a very gratifying conversation with a young minister from Ulster. Not only had he been converted in a crusade which it was my privilege to conduct in his hometown in 1955, but he assured me that one Presbyterian church there was still able to point to some ninety-five vigorous members who had confessed Christ during that mission.

"By their fruits ye shall know them." Converts of area-wide crusades should get socially involved and **provide together** for the misfortunes of others. So great was the fervor of the apostolic church that, following Pentecost, "all that believed were *together* and had all things common" (Acts 2:44). The form the new convert chooses to express his commitment to Christ must necessarily be between himself and his Lord. But the church in which he worships and serves ought to be very close to him in this matter. One man who was converted in Mr. Graham's Harringay Crusade became so concerned about the plight of the aged of England that he started a home for the elderly and by the time we were back in London in 1966, his Abbeyfield Homes numbered three hundred and they were all over Britain. George Adam Smith wrote of the Moody-Sankey Revival in Scotland that a generation later an objective observer could see the converts serving society in

almost any civic, social, ecclesiastical, or political arena into which
one might wish to look, and these were to be found not only in
their native Scotland but scattered around the world.

In this age of demonstrations and marches, converts of crusades—along with other Christians—will feel the urge to **protest
together**. "Let righteousness spring up *together,*" exhorted Isaiah
(45:8), and again, "Be dismayed and behold . . . *together*"
(41:23); yet again, "Let us come near *together* to judgment"
(41:1). Who is going to protest pornography, drunkenness, drug
addiction, crime, poverty, war mongering, and political corruption
in high places if Christians do not. Paul wrote to the Corinthians
that "God hath tempered the body *together*" (I Cor. 12:24); he
did not say He had put it together out of soft dough, but
"tempered" it together. In mid-1971, the Gallup Poll revealed that
90 percent of the American people believe that the barring of
Bible reading and prayers from public schools is a bad thing. Are
there no Christians willing to protest this ruling and gather support
to have the Supreme Court ruling reversed?

Finally, crusade converts will **praise God together**, both here
and with the saints of the ages, hereafter. Here they will "magni-
fy" and "exalt his name together" (Ps. 34:3). The day of conversion is always a glad day. When a lost sheep comes home, says
Jesus, the shepherd "calleth *together* his friends and neighbours,"
and they "rejoice" (Luke 15:6) in glad celebration. One day the
Chief Shepherd will appear and believers in Him "shall be caught
up *together* . . . to meet the Lord in the air" (I Thess. 4:17). Here
is the believer's greatest motivation: "we beseech you . . . by our
gathering *together* unto him" (II Thess. 2:1). When I was in
London in 1966, a critic asked me, "Where are the forty thousand
converts of the Billy Graham Harringay Crusade of 1954?" I
replied, "We meet them everywhere, in London, throughout
Britain, and as missionaries in every country which our team has
visited. But also, by the law of averages, eleven thousand of them
are already with Christ in glory, praising Jesus in such words as,
'unto Him that loved us, and washed us from our sins in His own
blood' (Rev. 1:5)."

Some impressions register indelibly on one's mind. I can never
forget, out on a hillside in southern Africa, as guest of Bishop
Stephen Bradley, Primate of the Church of England there, listening to a body of black Zulus sing:

We'll be dwelling together.
How happy we shall be throughout eternity,
For we'll be dwelling together,
My Lord and me.

On that day of jubilation, believers in Jesus, whether caught on the hook of a one-to-one fishing line, or in the net of a mass evangelistic crusade will be *together* with their Lord.

Let the Presses Roll 9

EVANGELISM THROUGH LITERATURE

Sherwood E. Wirt

Have you ever wished (while sitting through a dull sermon, perhaps) that you could read one written by Apollos who was "mighty in the Scriptures?" Have you ever wondered what kind of sermons Philip preached that brought such joy to Samaria? Luke gives both apostles high pulpit marks, but apparently no one took down what they said. The result is that their oratory is lost in the airwaves of antiquity. No one circulated their thoughts. No one handed a written copy of them to a friend. Apollos' eloquence echoed through the hills of Asia Minor and brought heaven closer to the listening believers, but he does nothing for us. Philip's proclamation brings no joy to the twentieth century. On the other hand, the Holy Spirit's preserving power enabled someone to record the passion of Peter and Paul and Stephen, so that today we are still being blessed and anointed as we read their messages in the New Testament.

A chapter on literature belongs either at the beginning or the ending of a volume on evangelism; at the beginning because the source of our faith is a literary source; at the end because when the preaching stops, the permanent work of literary evangelism begins. While our faith began historically with the spoken word in Galilee, and was borne and spread by oral witness, the Spirit of God chose a literary canon for the permanent extension of the gospel throughout the civilized world. "These [things] are written," as John said, "that ye might believe that Jesus is the Christ, the Son of God; and that believing ye might have life through his name" (John 20:31, KJV).

Today literary evangelism is still one of the most important channels open to us for conveying the good news. It may not raise a shout in the camp; it may not herald itself with a trumpet blast; but it works far more effectively than many Christians realize. A man may take home a book, cloth or paperback, or a tract, and read it in a moment of quiet. As a result he may be moved to reflect upon his life in a way which could be transforming. Yet that same man's inner defenses could perhaps never have been penetrated by a verbal proclamation. He perhaps would never walk near a church. The late Kenneth Strachan claimed that 85 percent of all Latin Americans who have come to Christ have been won by a book, a tract, a pamphlet, or some form of evangelical literature.

Whereas in Latin America there is a large demand and a small supply of evangelistic material, in North America the situation is reversed. There is a large supply and small demand, and for a very good reason. The supply is plentiful but much of it is mediocre. I would say that literary evangelism in the United States and Canada is being kept alive as if through a tracheal tube. The bite has gone out of the message, very few are chewing on it, and fewer still are swallowing. I know how desperate both religious and secular publishers are to get their hands on some vital, Bible-oriented, commitment-based evangelistic material that they can publish. If you walk into a Bible bookstore today, the chances are you will see not books but rather greeting cards, gifts, Scripture key-chains, and similar gimmickry. The books will often be hidden at the rear of the store on a wall shelf. But the bookstore manager is not to be censured; when you look at his book fare you will realize that much of the stock is written in such a pedestrian style that it is not worth reading.

The laymen and laywomen who make up the evangelical churches are vaguely aware of the deficiency, and in their own way they have taken steps to overcome it. In many churches circulating libraries have been established and stocked with reprints of spiritual messages by Andrew Murray, Charles Spurgeon and Dwight L. Moody. Probably the church librarian would like very much to have some good contemporary literature. He or she would like to stock some sermons by the church's own minister in book form, but the minister can't see it. He has several drawers full of sermons that he has preached, and some of them are very good, but he is usually too busy to prepare them for publication. Were he to send some of them to a magazine or to a publishing house, they might be accepted and he would reach a thousand times more people than he is currently addressing. But that kind of arithmetic confuses the preacher (he was never good at math anyway) so he lets it go.

Not every Christian leader feels that way, of course. In fact a dedicated corps of men and women are carrying on an astonishing and highly effective world-wide ministry of evangelism through literature. Consider the work of the various Bible Societies in publishing and distributing the Scriptures. Then too, a great literary thrust is being undertaken by the World Literature Crusade, Evangelical Literature Overseas, Wycliffe Translators, the Christian Literature Crusade, the Pocket Testament League, the Laubach Literacy effort, and other agencies. The publishing arms of the various denominational and interdenominational agencies, and the publishers of various Christian books, paperbacks, magazines, periodicals, pamphlets, and tracts, are all engaged full time in producing Christian literature. The material they circulate is sometimes excellent, and usually is produced with serious intent and the highest motivation. Yet quality is not always its chief characteristic, and it is not because of a lack of funds. After all, they can only print and distribute what the writers write.

It is one thing to criticize the literary output, another to try to correct it. In recent months I have visited thirteen countries and conducted a dozen writing schools, seminars, and clinics all over the South Pacific, the Orient, and western Europe. My firm conviction is that we are not developing writing talent for our generation to convey effectively the gospel. Our young people read and re-read C. S. Lewis, and ask "Where are the Lewises of today?" In Australia, in Indonesia, in Singapore, in Taiwan, in Hong Kong, in the Philippines, and in Japan I met with writers who are fully able to present the gospel to this generation, but they have not learned how to polish their prose and they do not know where the editors are. In Europe I found plenty of good writers and publishers, but considerable confusion about the nature of evangelism. Nowhere did I find a dedicated school of young writers utterly committed to Jesus Christ and ready to lay their typewriters at His feet.

In America my work often takes me to college campuses, and

the young Christian leaders who have invited me take pains to inform me about the evangelistic activity taking place among the students. I learn about the dormitory prayer groups, the meetings of the Fellowship of Christian Athletes, the periodic visits to living houses, the chapel programs, the denominational student centers, the nearby churches, the Bible study groups, and the ski trips. I even learn about evangelistic literature that is printed locally and distributed on and off campus.

Then I ask, "How many Christians are on the staff of the campus daily newspaper or the literary journal that everyone reads? How many Christians are working in the college bookstores that everyone visits?" I draw a blank. It is a fact that these institutions are often staffed by people who are neutral, if not hostile, to the gospel. Yet here are the vital media that constitute the effective instruments of campus opinion and shape and re-shape student thinking.

God does not discriminate between methods of evangelism; he uses them all. Paul said that he rejoiced in every way that Christ was preached, and so should we. If there are tribespeople in the upper reaches of the Orinoco River who have not heard the gospel, we should send our young missionaries up there to reach them. But I also have a feeling that God is concerned about what is happening in the communications explosion. I believe we should be training young men and women to become good writers and journalists, and then catapulting them into the mass media. They should be infiltrating especially the field of written communications, taking over posts of leadership not by craftiness but by craft; not by supernatural intervention so much as by the fact that they are the best in the business. What could God do, for example, with a dedicated Christian columnist today; or with a Christian TV commentator? In the increasing chaos of our exploding society, think of the need for wisdom, for profundity, for depth of analysis. Think of the need for a Christian understanding of men and events, for a Biblical point of view that nails sin for what it is, and points to a solution that draws on all the resources of the universe.

Is this too much to expect? Is there anywhere in the journalistic or literary field an evangelical capable of such an assignment? I say there are a lot of people who are *capable of being capable* of such a role. A good example of a late-blooming writer for Christ would be Malcolm Muggeridge, the British journalist whose best-known

attributes are a ready wit and an acid tongue. Muggeridge has
blown up a storm in the world of letters by (if I may borrow his
term) rediscovering Jesus Christ. He is a sometime editor of *Punch,*
sometime chancellor of Edinburgh University, and a darling of
BBC television. Now he is shaking the caps off the teeth of the
media people, forcing them to take a fresh look at the claims of
One who said He was the Light and Savior of the world.

Muggeridge's gift for analysis and expression is such that he is
able to bend and mold the thinking of thousands if not millions of
people. Because he is such a persuasive writer, his new love for the
Lord has encouraged believers and given hope to seekers. He is
making the kind of impact, in short, that I believe God is expect-
ing of every writing man and woman who places his talent on the
sacred altar. He illustrates my conviction that there is no limit to
the outreach, influence or effectiveness of the Christian writer
who is prepared to train himself and to make himself available as a
servant of God's Word. We should never forget that it was a
journalist, Karl Marx, who changed the face of the world while
sitting at a chair in the British Museum—writing.

If I am partial to the written language as an instrument of
communication it is because I have learned to appreciate its
qualities of availability and permanence. Marshall McLuhan, the
Canadian sage, has tried to bury the linear age, as he calls it, or the
Gutenberg age. He thinks we are moving swiftly into the electric
age, when knowledge will be dispensed primarily through the
audio-visual media. Reading and books are about finished, he says.
Strangely, he had to write a book to tell us about his ideas; and
that is just the point. Prose may not have the dramatic qualities of
a telecast, but prose is available when we want it, where we can
find it. Prose furthermore has to stand on its own merits. It cannot
lean for effect on a pointing finger or a dramatic pause or an
inflection in the voice. And prose will be around for some time to
come. The voice of the preacher dies out; the stirring radio
broadcast signs off; the epochal magnetic tape disintegrates; the
religious films rot in their cans; but a book about Jesus Christ will
last for centuries.

Good writing is a cultural achievement. It probably stands
higher in the scale of civilization than any other form of communication except the fine arts. It provides a magnificent medium for
the transmission of ideas. But what is good writing? It is not a
calling, for God calls the whole man and not just his typewriter. It

is not a trade or a profession, for very few men ply it successfully. It is not a hobby, for it absorbs more attention than any hobby should. It is not a gift, as a singing voice is a gift, for very few writers are truly gifted. Huckleberry Finn told it "like it is" when he said, "There ain't nothin' more to write about, and I am rotten glad of it, because if I'd a-knowed what a trouble it was to make a book I wouldn't a-tackled it, and ain't a-going to no more."

Good writing (and here is my point) is neither a calling nor a trade, nor a hobby, nor a gift; it is a *craft*. It is a craft demanding skill achieved through hours and years of toil and diligent application to the disciplines involved. A man learns sculpturing by chipping marble, and woodcarving by wielding a knife; just as he learns to write by writing. The elements for mastery of the craft are powers of observation, objectivity, and honesty on the one hand, and a willingness to allow one's work to be improved on the other.

Whether a person is a top-flight Christian author does not depend upon his appearance, his charm, his skin-color, his bankbook, his status, his age, his ancestry, or his sex. It does depend, more than most of us realize, on his willingness to consult the dictionary and synonym finder, to seek out friendly and dependable critics, and to rewrite his own material. And because writing is the most democratic of all crafts, the zealous Christian who feels ineffective before cameras and microphones can be greatly used of God through the written word to win thousands to the Savior.

Part of the problem of many Christian writers is their attachment to the past. They write the way their mothers wrote. Style plays a large part in communication; and tomorrow's religious book will be tightly written. It will be factual and realistic; it will tell the situation as it is; it will seek to reproduce succinctly on paper what people are seeing and hearing on their screens and already know to be the case. It will document its claims. That does not mean that the Christian writer is doomed to reporting minutiae and irrelevata; far from it. Instead, when the Christian message is written, it will be set out in straightforward fashion, without bloomers or petticoats, without lofty phrases or purple passages, colorfully yet simply, in language that is chaste and that moves purposefully to its point.

The author of the seventies who will evangelize effectively will be a person who knows the English language and the writers who have mastered it. Journalism courses are valuable, but they are no substitute for a grasp of Geoffrey Chaucer, William Shakespeare, John Milton, John Bunyan, Jonathan Swift, Samuel Johnson, Robert Browning, or even Ernest Hemingway. To live in the twentieth century and to understand it, one must not only know these men; one must also know Sören Kierkegaard, Karl Marx and Fyodor Dostoevsky. There is no easy way to master such men; if we haven't read them, we haven't read them, and sooner or later our bluff will be called. And may I add that I feel there is very little God can do with a lazy Christian writer. This is an age with an explosion of human knowledge; and the evangelistic writer cannot afford to bypass it, or to ignore what the whole world is aware of. The Christian author who speaks to the modern world will need to know not only his Shakespeare and his Marx, but also his Augustine, his Luther, his Wesley, his Karl Barth, and his Carl Henry. He does not need to be a seminary man, but if he is, he should choose the finest, most Biblically-centered seminary in the country.

What I have been saying is that the man who is going to evangelize through books and literature has to be more than an evangelist. The best way I can describe him is to call him a Renaissance-Reformation man. Who is the Renaissance man? He is the man not of encyclopedic knowledge so much as encyclopedic interest. He is the connoisseur, even the dilettante. He is the William Buckley type who seems comfortably at home in any field of human inquiry, the George Plimpton type who is game for anything. He is the man of wide-ranging interest, of polish, of sophistication, of manners, of taste, of humor. He makes strong points in a gentle, telling manner. He is civilized; he does not "lose his cool." He knows his history, his languages, his poets, his scientists, his sports. He is one of the beautiful people, cultured, cultivated, educated, charming.

By way of contrast I would oppose to him the Reformation man. This man comes as it were from the same period of history, but he is different. The Reformation man is a man of God's Book. He is a man of unrelenting purpose and moral passion, a man with the gleam of eternity in his eye. He is a buttonholer for Christ. He is looking for revival in the church. His aim is not to go forward so much as to go back—back to the first century, back to the time when God revealed Himself in the spoken Word. The Reformation man is a man not of pleasantries but of action. He is God's prophet. He proclaims the gospel of Jesus Christ, the glad tidings of great joy. He also pierces men's consciences, warns men of hell and judgment, and bids them repent and be saved. To him literature is a tool provided by God, to be used while there is time before the end, by the Holy Spirit, to draw men into the Kingdom.

Both of these streams entered our civilization about the same time, in the fifteenth and sixteenth centuries; and as historians have pointed out, our modern society has witnessed almost the complete triumph of the Renaissance over the Reformation. I believe that the Christian author today should seek to combine the Renaissance man and the Reformation man. We cannot do without the one or the other. As an illustration of this combination, consider the apostle Paul. As Renaissance Man, he quoted the Greek poets Epimenides and Menander; as Reformation Man, Paul quoted Isaiah, Moses, and David. Paul told the people of Corinth, "I am become all things to all men, so that by all means I might save some." That is the Renaissance man speaking. But he also said to the same congregation, "I determined to know nothing among you save Jesus Christ and him crucified." That is the Reformation man speaking.

I say the Christian evangelistic writer should be a Renaissance man who knows more about culture and history and custom than the skeptic alongside him. He should know more about this world even though he doesn't belong to this world and he is looking for a better world. But as a Reformation man he should be committed to what Dr. John A. Mackay calls "the majesty of truth." The Christian church stands or falls on its belief that the Bible is truth. And what does the Bible say that is true? It says that man is a sinner and that God can save him for eternity in Jesus Christ. So as a Reformation man the Christian should be writing about salvation, the cross, the new birth, the empty tomb, forgiveness of sin, the baptism of the Spirit, justification by faith, sanctifying power, the priesthood of believers, and freedom in Christ. These are the themes that can change men and turn them from darkness to light.

Our Lord is waiting for Christian writers who will win their way into places of strategy and influence by their ability to put words together in provocative and interesting ways, and who will place their craftmanship at the disposal of the Holy Spirit. The great reading public is waiting for evangelical writers who will make sense, who will articulate their minds, who will relate the eternal truths of the Bible to the modern scene.

God did commit to us the saving message of the gospel. Christian writers should not be religious hacks, trying to milk the public with a special brand of esoteric teaching. Christians are servants of truth, stewards of the mysteries of grace, vessels of mud, commissioned to carry the divine treasure. They are told not to throw this treasure to the swine, but to offer it to men. I believe that literature is the one great untapped resource of the evangelical in his desire to reach lost men for Jesus Christ.

Have You Caught the Spirit?

THE SPIRIT OF EVANGELISM

10

Ralph G. Turnbull

The question may be asked, "Why another book on evangelism?" Many available books have assisted pastors and members of churches in their work of evangelism. However, recent events point to a reawakened interest in evangelism and this book may well encourage a new generation in our Lord's commission to bring the good news to all people. Indicating a new interest in presenting the good news, several conferences have been held in recent years:

1966—World Congress on Evangelism at Berlin.
1968—Far East Congress on Evangelism at Singapore.
1969—American Congress on Evangelism at Minneapolis.
1971—European Congress on Evangelism at Amsterdam.

These were convened under the auspices of the Billy Graham Evangelistic Association. Other groups and churches have held or plan to hold similar gatherings:

1970—Evangelicals met at Key West to plan for the future.
1971—"Good News," the forum for Scriptural Christianity within the United Methodist Church, attracted 1,800 delegates to Cincinnati.
1971—The Celebration of Evangelism, sponsored by various Reformed and Presbyterian churches, was attended by 3,000 delegates.
1971—The Presbyterian Church of the United States began a three-year program.

103

1972—Campus Crusade for Christ is sponsoring a Congress on Evangelism in Dallas. One hundred thousand students are expected to attend.
1973—The Lutheran Church plans to emphasize evangelism during this year.
1973—"Key '73" is a year of special evangelistic efforts for many denominations.

All these programs point to a resurgence in evangelistic activity. Unrest on college campuses, ferment in society, racial tensions, the drug menace, crime and anarchy in our cities, and lowered morals in a permissive age—all point to the urgent need for effective evangelistic programs.

God calls us again to evangelism. But what is the message from God to man? Films, novels, drama, music, art, radio, and television affect multitudes, but what is the truth? The late William Temple gave a description of evangelism which is still valid. He said, "Evangelism is the winning of men to acknowledge Christ as their Savior and King, so that they may give themselves to His service in the fellowship of His Church." Daniel T. Niles of Ceylon said that evangelism was simply the missionary task of the church and "one beggar sharing with another beggar."

The spirit of evangelism should be seen in terms of the great commission given by our Lord (Matt. 28:19, 20), in the context of the parable of the finding of the lost sheep (Luke 15), and in the realism of the parable of the four types of soil (Matt. 13). The variety of emphases found in this book should not blind us to the fact that behind all methods and techniques there is the content and theme of the evangel. We must share the good news with the world; the evangelist must spend his strength as an advocate and as a witness. All Christians are called to this task. This book should help both the pastor, in his role as leader, and the members of the congregation as they carry out this ministry.

There are two words which can help us understand the work before us—*overseer* and *pastor*. We watch, and we feed the flock of God. Using these concepts, John Milton spoke of false pastors and their failures. Referring to their ineffectiveness, he calls them "blind mouths." Milton adds, "The hungry sheep look up, and are not fed." This is an indictment that is still true. In the words *blind mouths* Milton combines a criticism of the work of the pastor and teacher. He is to watch over the flock, but fails, so Milton calls him "blind." He is to feed the sheep, but fails again, so Milton says

instead of doing that he is trying to be fed himself, thus he is a
"mouth." In this light we seek to understand the evangelism of the
pastor.

The time is ripe for a restudy of this crucial subject. For several
decades, the word *evangelism* was held in some disrepute. It was
associated with outdated methods, unattractive theology, and un-
ethical handling of money. In recent years, however, various
denominations have gradually returned to an awareness of the
need for evangelism. This resurgence is due partly to the fact that
churches are finding it more difficult to win adherents and converts. For some time, proselytism and conversions were under
suspicion because of a false theology of universalism which wel-
comed everyone without distinction. The nerve of evangelism had
been cut, but now a new mood prevails.

There was also a reaction against evangelism because of critical
assumptions about Charles G. Finney, Dwight L. Moody, or Billy
Graham. Since they represented traditional evangelism, they were
held up as examples of what we might avoid! Some charged that
these men diluted and confused the Christian message in their
methods and theology, even to the point of secularizing the
gospel. Some claimed that the social message of the gospel was
absent, except on issues like drink and gambling. Others suggested
that Finney opposed the abolition of slavery (which is not sub-
stantiated), that Moody was a social conformist, or that Graham
opposed desegregation until the Supreme Court, not the Holy
Spirit, told him it was wrong.

Some also charged that the evangelistic message "reduced sin to
simple, individualistic proportions." Others have said the social
dimensions of sin are being ignored and that revivalism makes
utopian claims. Such points of view have been found in all parts of
the Christian church.

The answer to the criticisms of yesterday is found in a renewed
interest in evangelism. The hour has come for Christians to re-
evaluate their commitment to this supreme task. Part of the
answer to the critics is to learn from them. Is there some truth to
their accusations? Has the main stream of the church been negli-
gent of social concerns in its ministry? Do we need reformation
and renewal rather than, or along with, revival and evangelism?
What is the mission of the church?

A partial answer can be found by noting that when Finney
preached and saw revival in his day, he also, through his *Lectures,*

inspired many reformers to fight for the abolition of slavery. Moody led many into YMCA work and united the efforts of Christians in dealing with social needs. Timothy L. Smith's notable book, *Revivalism and Social Reform,* documents the evidence that the evangelism and revivalism of another era in America played the key role in the widespread attack upon slavery, poverty, and greed. He claims that the social concerns of the church and the nation were not the product of socially-minded secularists, but the concern primarily of evangelical Christians. Great Britain likewise knew this thrust and aftermath of evangelism from the days of Moody. Thomas Chalmers began the movement in Scotland, and Moody inspired further advances. Earlier, England knew the profound influence of the Wesleys and the evangelical revival of the eighteenth century.

The impact of evangelism upon democratic life, political action, social concern, education, benevolence, and missionary outreach, as well as its encouragement of freedom of speech, religion, press, and gathering lay at the heart of progress. If there have been setbacks or aberrations, then let these be confessed; but let us not forget that the benefits to the churches and to society came because transformed people set to work in the renewal of the common life of those generations.

Some critics tell us that the day of the institutional church is past and that we must develop new forms of ministry. Structures and organizations from yesterday, so they say, are obsolete, and urgent situations seem to demand radical change.

Not so, says Bishop Bardsley of Conventry Cathedral in England, which was rebuilt after the bombing of World War II. Thousands have become involved in the program of the Cathedral: music, talks, lay projects, group meetings, films, art, architecture, symbolism, yes, and preaching. The spirit of evangelism had not died. The program at Coventry Cathedral is not that of a "professional." It is an example of a church and congregation pooling its strength to reach out into its community with a relevant program of evangelism.

This book points out that the key to evangelism is the evangelist, and he is found in both pastor and in people of every congregation. All varieties of evangelism are mentioned, and while techniques are not stressed, there is an unfolding of tried and sure ways from which all of us can learn. Evangelism begins not with methods, but with concerned people. Evangelism is a spirit to be caught. Our minds and hearts are captured by the love of Christ which constrains us to tell the good news. God is the seeking God. That is where evangelism begins. The cross was always in God's heart. Without that there could be no evangelism.

The aim of this book is to help readers catch this spirit. What other ages have experienced in personal conversions and social renewal will come again. The historian might well write of us and our generation what was written at the end of John Wesley's *Journal* in an attempt to account for his "warmed heart" and his evangelistic achievements:

> To one great purpose, he dedicated all his powers of body and mind; for this relinquished all honor and preferment. At all times and in all places, in season and out of season, by gentleness, by terror, by interest, by every motive and every inducement, he strove, with unwearied assiduity, to turn men from the error of their ways and awaken them to virtue and religion. To the bed of sickness or the couch of prosperity; to the prison or the hospital; to the house of mourning or the house of feasting, wherever there was a friend to serve or a soul to save, he readily repaired. He thought no office too humiliating, no condescension too low, no undertaking too arduous, to reclaim the meanest of God's offspring. The souls of men were equally precious in his sight.

In a day when preaching has been denigrated and other forms of ministry magnified, we do well to recall the lesson of history. When the church, through its representatives has proclaimed the good news and has had the authority of the Holy Spirit endorsing their message, history testifies to the forward thrust of Christianity throughout the world. Now is the time to recapture the glow of a vital preaching ministry. The age is one of disillusionment, and the good news is the answer to man's search for certitude and meaning.

In August, 1971, the Twelfth World Methodist Conference was held in Denver, Colorado. Dr. Alan Walker, President of the Methodist Conference of New South Wales, Australia, spoke on "Mission, the Priority of Ministry." In this address he reminded the leaders of Methodism that " . . . the message to be proclaimed while on mission is all-important. Methods, techniques of mission have their place, yet too often when turning to evangelism, we think of the means of communication rather than the communication to be given. We might as well ask, What shall it profit a church, a ministry, if it perfects its techniques and has nothing to say? . . . There is one word to be said about the ways the message of the gospel is to be communicated. It is by many means, but at the head of the list I would place preaching. A believing church will be a preaching church."

If preaching were restored to its former state and given honor again in all our churches, we would witness a renewal of vital Christianity. The fault for the decline in the church lies in the downgrading of the Christian message, and here the pulpit must take the responsibility. A strong pulpit makes a strong church. A convinced preacher compels a congregation to rise up in its mission. Evangelism is the outreach and missionary thrust of the church. Our Lord gave this the highest place in His ministry and teaching. During His teaching He made His disciples understand that there was a harvest of people ready for their reaping. At the climax of His ministry He reiterated the same in His commission to the disciples to go into all the world and evangelize, making disciples. Whether in personal contact, city-wide influence, national witness, or international proclamation, the gospel was sent out as good news to a needy world.

The spirit of evangelism must be caught once more. Concern and compassion must fill our hearts. Against the background of eternity, the Christian sees life whole and steady. Because God has broken through into our human dimensions, the good news of the abundant life is the one hope for this life and the life to come. All the false gods pass away. Only the one true and living God remains. In the world's darkness of disbelief "the light still shines in the darkness, and the darkness has never put it out" (John 1:5, Phillips). Charles S. Duthie, Principal of New College, London has said:

> We are the inheritors of a great gospel. We have no need to be ashamed of it. The church is still the agent and the servant of that gospel. We are not called upon to abandon it but to let the mercy and power of God flow through it to men. It is a gospel to be shared with the whole world.

Sometimes the reading of selected Scriptures or a choice poem will stir the mind and imagination and thrust us out into the arena of need with the glad tidings. Pastors and people together can find stimulus and good cheer in their common task from the words of *Saint Paul,* by Frederic W. H. Myers:

> Christ! I am Christ's! and let the name suffice you,
> Ay, for me too He greatly hath sufficed;

Lo with no winning words I would entice you,
Paul has no honor and no friend but Christ.

. . . .

Oh could I tell, ye surely would believe it!
Oh could I only say what I have seen!
How should I tell or how can ye receive it,
How, till He bringeth you where I have been?

. . . .

Whoso has felt the Spirit of the Highest
Cannot confound nor doubt Him nor deny;
Yea with one voice, O world, tho' thou deniest,
Stand thou on that side, for on this am I.

. . . .

Yea, thro' life, death, thro' sorrow and thro' sinning
He shall suffice me, for He hath sufficed:
Christ is the end, for Christ was the beginning,
Christ the beginning, for the end is Christ.

The marching orders of the Lord come through in our day
clearly. In that framework, there can be no argument or dispute
concerning the work of evangelism. The lost must be found; the
dead must be raised; the deaf must hear; the blind must see. The
Lord's own mandate read: "The Spirit of the Lord is upon me,
because he hath anointed me to preach the gospel to the poor; he
hath sent me to heal the brokenhearted, to preach deliverance to
the captives, and recovering of sight to the blind, to set at liberty
them that are bruised, To preach the acceptable year of the Lord"
(Luke 4:18, 19, KJV). This is not merely a task given us to do: it
is our life-blood, for only by it do we live. Pray then for the
enlightened mind to know, the warmed heart to feel, and the
willing feet to act.

Bibliography

Allan, Tom, *The Face of My Parish*. London: S.C.M. Press, 1954.

Barclay, William. *Turning to God: A Study of Conversion in the Book of Acts and Today*. 1964. Reprint. Grand Rapids: Baker Book House, 1972.

Barlow, Walter. *God So Loved: The Spiritual Basis of Evangelism*. New York: Fleming H. Revell Co., 1952.

Brandon, Owen. *Christianity from Within: A Frank Discussion of Religion, Conversion, Evangelism and Revival*. London: Hodder & Stoughton, 1965.

Brown, Fred. *Secular Evangelism*. London: S.C.M. Press, 1970.

Brown, J. A. C. *Techniques of Persuasion*. Baltimore: Penguin Books, 1963.

Cone, James. *Black Theology and Black Power*. New York: Seabury Press, 1969.

Cook, Henry. *The Theology of Evangelism: The Gospel in the World of Today*. London: Carey-Kingsgate Press, 1951.

De Blank, Joost. *The Parish in Action*. New York: Morehouse-Gorham Co., 1954.

Dillistone, F. W. *Revelation and Evangelism*. London: Lutterworth Press, 1948.

Falconer, R. H. W. *Success and Failure of a Radio Mission*. London: S.C.M. Press, 1951.

Ford, Leighton. *The Christian Persuader*. New York: Harper & Row, 1960.

————. *Evangelism: The Church's Task in a Changing World*. Minneapolis: Billy Graham Association, 1965.

Grand Rapids Board of Evangelism of the Christian Reformed

Churches. *Reformed Evangelism: A Manual on Principles and Methods of Evangelization.* Grand Rapids: Baker Book House, 1962.

Green, Bryan. *The Practice of Evangelism.* London: Hodder & Stoughton, 1951.

Green, Peter. *Fishers of Men.* London: A. R. Mowbray & Co., 1953.

Henry, Carl F. H. *A Plea for Evangelical Demonstration.* Grand Rapids: Baker Book House, 1971.

Kuiper, R. B. *God-Centered Evangelism: A Presentation of the Scriptural Theology of Evangelism.* Grand Rapids: Baker Book House, 1961.

Misselbrook, L. R. *Winning the People for Christ: An Experiment in Evangelism.* London: Carey-Kingsgate Press, 1956.

Niles, D. T. *That They May Have Life.* London: Lutterworth Press, 1952.

Packer, James I. *Evangelism and the Sovereignty of God.* London: Inter-Varsity Fellowship, 1961.

Ramage, Ian. *Battle for the Free Mind.* London: George Allen & Unwin, 1967.

Rees, Paul S. *Stir Up the Gift.* Grand Rapids: Zondervan Publishing House, 1962.

Routley, Erik. *The Gift of Conversion.* London: Lutterworth Press, 1957.

Sargent, William. *Battle for the Mind.* London: Heinemann, 1957.

Scharpff, Paulus. *History of Evangelism: Three Hundred Years of Evangelism in Germany, Great Britain, and the United States of America.* Grand Rapids: William B. Eerdmans Publishing Co., 1964.

Stewart, James S. *A Faith to Proclaim.* London: Hodder & Stoughton, 1953.

Stott, John R. W. *Our Guilty Silence.* London: Hodder & Stoughton, 1967.

Stowe, David M. *Ecumenicity and Evangelism.* Grand Rapids: William B. Eerdmans Publishing Co., 1970.

Sweazey, George E. *Effective Evangelism: The Greatest Work in the World.* New York: Harper & Brothers, 1953.

Taylor, J. Randolph. *God Loves Like That! The Theology of James Denney.* London: S.C.M. Press, 1962.

Taylor, Vincent. *Doctrine and Evangelism.* London: Epworth Press, 1953.

Temple, William. *Towards the Conversion of England.* London: Lambeth Conference Report, 1954.

Thomson, D. P. *Aspects of Evangelism.* Crieff, Scotland: Research Unit, 1968.

Trumbull, Charles G. *Taking Men Alive: Studies in the Principle and Practice of Individual Soul-Winning.* New York: Association Press, 1917.

Turnbull, Ralph G. *The Preacher's Heritage, Task, and Resources.* Grand Rapids: Baker Book House, 1968.

Webster, Douglas. *What Is Evangelism?* London: The Highway Press, 1959.

Wedel, Theo. O. *A Theological Reflection on the Work of Evangelism.* New York: World Council of Churches, 1959.

Williams, Colin W. *For the World: A Study Book in Evangelism.* New York: National Council of Churches, 1965.

Wirt, Sherwood E. *The Social Conscience of the Evangelical.* New York: Harper & Row, 1968.

Wolf, Carl J. C., ed. *Jonathan Edwards on Evangelism.* Grand Rapids: William B. Eerdmans Publishing Co., 1958.